Meditations on the Life and Passion of Christ

Early English Text Society.

Original Series, No. 158.

1921 (for 1919).

Meditations on the Life and Passion of Christ

FROM

BRITISH MUSEUM ADDIT. MS. 11307

BY

CHARLOTTE D'EVELYN, Ph.D.

LONDON:
PUBLISHED FOR THE EARLY ENGLISH TEXT SOCIETY
BY HUMPHREY MILFORD, OXFORD UNIVERSITY PRESS
AMEN CORNER, E.C. 4.

OXFORD
UNIVERSITY PRESS

Great Clarendon Street, Oxford OX2 6DP
United Kingdom

Oxford University Press is a department of the University of Oxford.
It furthers the University's objective of excellence in research, scholarship,
and education by publishing worldwide. Oxford is a registered trade mark of
Oxford University Press in the UK and in certain other countries

© The Early English Text Society 1921

The moral rights of the authors have been asserted

Database right Oxford University Press (maker)

First Edition published in 1921

All rights reserved. No part of this publication may be reproduced,
stored in a retrieval system, or transmitted, in any form or by any means,
without the prior permission in writing of Oxford University Press,
or as expressly permitted by law, or under terms agreed with the appropriate
reprographics rights organization. Enquiries concerning reproduction
outside the scope of the above should be sent to the Rights Department,
Oxford University Press, at the address above

You must not circulate this book in any other form
and you must impose this same condition on any acquirer

Published in the United States of America by Oxford University Press
198 Madison Avenue, New York, NY 10016, United States of America

British Library Cataloguing in Publication Data
Data available

Library of Congress Cataloging in Publication Data
Data available

Original Series, 158

ISBN 978-0-85-991898-5

TABLE OF CONTENTS

                                                                      PAGE

INTRODUCTION—

    I. MS. AND DIALECT vii
        1. Introductory vii
        2. MS. viii
        3. Dialect ix
    II. SUMMARY AND SOURCES OF THE *MEDITATIONS* . xv
        1. Summary xv
        2. The *Orison of the Passion* . . . xxii
        3. Richard Rolle xxv
        4. The *Bible* xxx
        5. Hugo of St. Victor xxxiii

TEXT OF THE *MEDITATIONS* 1

APPENDIX: TEXT OF THE *ORISON* . . . 60

INDEX OF PROPER NAMES 65

GLOSSARY 66

INTRODUCTION

I. THE MS. AND ITS DIALECT

1. INTRODUCTORY

THE poem which is printed for the first time in the following pages might be described briefly as a compendium of the lyric themes of Middle English religious poetry. One may find within it passages representing the hymn of praise in honour of the Virgin (vv. 79 f.), and the prayer asking for her intercession (vv. 2162 f.); or, again, meditations on the incidents of the Passion expressed in simple, devout language (vv. 489 f. and 1527 f.), or elaborated into series of rhetorical conceits (vv. 1829 f.). There are many passages typical of the lyric of love-longing (vv. 683 f., 807 f., and 1289 f.), and even the moral ballade is represented in substance in lines on the transitoriness of human life (vv. 2187 f.). These themes all grow out of the poet's contemplation of different incidents of the life of Christ; hence the poem has been given the title, *Meditations on the Life and Passion of Christ*.[1]

The poem is a fairly late production. The appearance in this text of passages from Richard Rolle[2] establishes the probable *terminus a quo* of its composition. Rolle died in 1349; it is not likely, therefore, that the *Meditations* was composed very long before the middle of the fourteenth century, and perhaps more likely that it belongs to the second half of that century. Furthermore, the poet makes use of another poem, *An Orison of the Passion*,[3] which is not found in

---

[1] There is no title in the MS. The poem might be appropriately called *A Praising of Christ and the Virgin* in the manner of a somewhat similar meditation in prose, *A Talkyng of the Love of God* (printed by Horstmann, *Richard Rolle of Hampole*, London, 1895, II, p. 345 f.). The poet always speaks of his work as a *praising;* as for instance in his opening lines, addressed to Christ (v. 3): *Of þe I make þis praysyng;* and in the closing lines, spoken to Mary (v. 2248): *Wiþ þis preysyng I þe grete.* The title chosen, however, has the advantage of giving a more definite idea of the contents of the poem.

[2] See p. xxvii. below.   [3] See p. xxiv. below, and the Appendix.

MSS. earlier than the second half of the same century, a fact which gives another bit of evidence for assigning the *Meditations* to that period. The *terminus ad quem* is the first half of the fifteenth century, the date of the only MS. in which the *Meditations* is preserved.[1] There is no evidence, so far discovered, upon which a more definite date can be established.

The *Meditations*, as we have suggested, is not a single poem, but a collection of lyric themes loosely bound together. The material of some of these distinct passages is not new; it has been incorporated into the present text with little or no change, from other writings, both Latin and English. These borrowings, wherever they have been detected, are discussed in the following pages, as indications of the author's literary affiliations. His work, in spite of such borrowings, is essentially original, and in some of its passages stands comparison with the best lyric expression of Middle English literature.

2. THE MANUSCRIPT

The *Meditations* is preserved in one MS., Brit. Mus. Addit. 11307, a vellum octavo dating from the first half of the fifteenth century.[2] The poem in question, which is the first article in the MS., covers folios 7a–87b, and is interleaved with a modern transcription made by Joseph Haslewood in the early years of the nineteenth century. His title—the poem has none in the MS.—reads, *On the Birth, Death and Resurrection of Our Savior*. The poem numbers 2254 lines, not 2252, as the catalogue states. The MS. is neatly written, with a few capitals in red and the first letters of each line stroked in red. Occasionally paragraph divisions are indicated by a red mark, but otherwise there is no break in the text. Two other religious poems, *The Charter of Christ*,[3] and *The Dialogue between the Virgin and St. Bernard*,[4] complete the contents of this MS.[5]

[1] See the following section.
[2] See *List of the Add. to the MSS. in the Brit. Mus. in the Years 1836–1840*, London, 1843, p. 2, of additions for 1838. The catalogue gives the fifteenth century as the date of the MS.; a pencilled note signed F.M. dates it "in the reign of Henry the Sixth or perhaps earlier." See M. C. Spalding, *Middle English Charters of Christ*, Bryn Mawr, 1914, p. xxx, where the date is given as the first half of the fifteenth century on the authority of Sir George Warner.
[3] Printed by Miss Spalding, *op. cit.*, p. 18 f.
[4] See E.E.T.S. o. s. 98, p. 297 for the same poem printed from the Vernon MS.
[5] Haslewood adds in an Appendix transcriptions of four other poems, and a glossarial index; see Carleton Brown, *A Register of Middle English Religious and Didactic Verse*, Oxford, 1916, I, p. 392.

Introduction ix

3. DIALECT

The dialect of MS. Addit. 11307, is clearly south Midland. Its variations from normal Midland forms usually show southern influence,[1] while Northern colouring is rare. There is no decisive evidence, however, for determining whether the dialect is of the east or the west part of the south Midland.[2]

As a scribal peculiarity should be noted the extensive use of *on* for the usual *en* in final unaccented syllables. *On* appears as the ending of the infinitive (see *prayson* 8, *tellon* 83, *falwon* 110), as the ending of the third person plural, present, and preterite (see *shulon* 110, *clepon* 543, *knelon* 1048, *eton* 260), and as the ending of the past participles of strong verbs (see *comon* 143, *fallon* 289, *writon* 329). Another peculiarity, which appears only rarely, however, is the form *maud(e)* used for *maid* and *made* (see 9, 16, 262, 1693, 1796). Again, in several words *i* has been written for *g* or *ȝ*; as in *scories* 634, 1392, 1553, 1750, for *scorges*, which appears in this latter spelling only twice, 528, 1339. *Charied* 989, is evidently intended for *charged*, and *chanyeth*, 1746, with *y* instead of *i*, for *changeth*. þ and ð are frequently interchanged (see *þeth* for *deth* 823 and *þet* for *deþ* 371; *clodeþ* for *cloþed* 940; *þrynk* for *drynk* 995; *de* for *þe* 922; *suffred* for *suffreþ* 319; *defes* for *þeþes* 1792).[3] Otherwise the spellings in this MS. are not unusually inconsistent or careless.

That the dialect of this MS. is south Midland, as stated above, will be evident from the results of the following tests. Several of the applied tests do not distinguish the Midland definitely from the Southern dialect, but such tests serve at least to show the absence of Northern characteristics, and to strengthen the evidence furnished by the definite Midland tests.[4]

1. O.E. *ā* 7 *ō* in the Midland and South; *no* 8; *holy gost* 14; *so*

---

[1] See forms cited under Nos. 4, 7, 8, 10, 15, below.

[2] West Midland use of *u* in unaccented end syllables appears in two words, in *nakud* 1517; and in *lengur* 220, in which the *u* may be doubtful, since it is indicated only by a curl. See Morsbach, *Mittelenglische Grammatik*, Halle, 1896, p. 15. In *The Charter of Christ* preserved in this MS. (see notes 2 and 3, p. x.), three examples of this usage occur; *nakud* 90, *selus* 135, *helud* 160. These forms suggest slight west Midland influence. Again, the southern influence most noticeable in our text is that of the south-west (see test No. 4), so that the dialect shows a slight leaning towards the west of the south Midland district.

[3] See in *The Charter of Christ*, *þronke* for *dronke* 166, *þar* for *dar* 212; this continued confusion of þ and ð suggests that these forms are due to the scribe rather than to the MS. he was copying; unless, indeed, these two poems were both taken from a MS. in which this confusion already existed.

[4] Lists of dialectical distinctions are given in Morsbach, *Gram.*, p. 18 f. and in Kaluza, *Hist. Gram. der engl. Sprache*, 2nd part, Berlin, 1901, p. 12 f.

x   *Introduction*

22; *more* 43; *wroth* 135; *bon* 286; *wot* 333; *hol* 408; *rore* 518; *po* 602; *mon* 612; *lore* 679; *tokenynge* 713; *wrot* 883; *clopes* 964; *fo* 1378. An exception occurs in *stan* used in the compound *stannaked* 1762. This may be merely a scribal error, perhaps occasioned by the immediately preceding *stand*. In *namore* 1280, 2050, and in the indefinite article *an* 781, etc., the unaccented *a* has been shortened; in *halwen* 1779, the following consonant group has shortened the vowel.[1]

In the case of O.E. *ā* + *w, g,* the MS. shows variation between *a* and *o;* in rime *law*:*gnawe* 213; *ydrawe*:*yslawe* 251; *lawes*:*felawes* 1793; *i-knowe*:*crowe* 757; *lowe*:*knowe* 1267; *prowe*:*rowe* 269; and within the line, *drawen* 1021; *drawe* 380; *snow* 758; *knowyng* 1008; *saule* 220, 1642, and *soules* 234. The form *slayn* (see 280, 288, 903, etc.), is found more frequently within the line than the *slawe(n)* forms used in rime.[2]

2. W.S. *ǣ* (from Germanic *ā*) before *r* gives *a* in the North, *o* and *e* in the Midland, and *e* in the South: *were* 13, 15, 25, etc.; *per(e)* 106, 114, 147, 192, etc.; *where* 142, 249, etc.; *er* 320; *ber(e)* 746, 838, 860; *bere* (2nd sing. pret.) 682. The single exception is *whar-to* 1689. There are no examples of Midland *ō* developed from Northern *ā*, so that here again the MS. shows closer connection with the South than with the North. With one exception, this *e* rimes only with *ę̄*; *dere*:*were* 973; *spere*:*were* 1577; *cler*[3]:*per* 1101; *ber*:*maner* 745; *chere*:*were* 1933. The exception, a rime with *ę̣̄*, is *pere*:*ere* 241.

3. W.S. *ea* before *ld* appears as *ā* in the North, *ō* in the Midland and in the South, with the exception of Kent, which has *ē*:*holden* 248; *folde* 645; *colde* 646, 1183; *hundredfold* 1184; *olde* 1253, 1736; *tolden* 1739; *sold* 1472; *bold* 2074. No exceptions to Midland usage appear.

4. O.E. *ỹ* 7 *ĭ* (*y*) in the North and Midland, *ŭ* in the South-west, *ē* in Kent. This MS. shows all three forms, sometimes for the same word.

(*a*) with *i* (*y*): *clipte* 153; *myrthes* 164, *myrpe* 971; *stydefast* 317; *kisseth* 391; *sinne* 430; *hiddon* 454; *pinketh* 559; *fulfilt* 867; *fyr* 869; *fir* 1321; *litel, lytel* 889, 495, 394; *michel* 968; *mykel* 22, 49;

---

[1] See Kaluza, *Gram.*, p. 24, § 210 b.
[2] The *aw, au* forms are cited as Northern and Kentish: see Morsbach, *Gram.*, p. 13, No. 3, and p. 22, No. 3; Kaluza, *Gram.* p. 12, § 204. l. Since our MS. belongs to the south rather than to the north Midland, it is probably influenced by the Kentish rather than by the Northern *aw* forms.
[3] For the sound of *e* in romance words, see Kaluza, *Gram.*, p. 62, § 237.

Introduction

myrie 972, 1773; *gylt* 1253; *gilt* 1872; *hidynge* 1401; *þrist* 1782; *ʒit* 889.

(*b*) with *e*: *dede* (3rd sing. pret: this is the only form used), 104, 504, etc.; *keste* 153; *wercheth* 334; *lesteneþ* 889; *werse* 1212, 1810; *ferste* 1261; *leste* 1580; *werkes* 1809; *helle* 1843; *helles* 1844; *stedefast* 2064; *ʒet* 1129, 1374.

(*c*) with *u*: *forthfulle* 7; *mukel* 293, 1498, etc; *muchel* 2135; *burde* 166; *hud* 456, 1772; *muche* 664, 1554, etc.; *such* 873, 1531; *purst* 996; *apurst* 1576, 1781; *murþe* 1071; *ykuste* 1179; *put* 1255, 1842; *shut* 1841; *gurd* 1321; *þruste* 1579; *brunye* 1591; *stude* 1601; *cluppyng* 1645; *kussyng* 1645; *fulþe* 2025; *ykud* 2163; *yhud* 2164; *ʒut* 1787.

The following words in the above lists show the three forms: *stydefast, stedefast, stude; kisseth, keste, ykusted; ʒit, ʒet, ʒut*. This intermixture with normal Midland forms, of *e* and *u* forms which suggest Kentish and south-western influence respectively, could occur most easily in the south Midland. London documents, for instance, show a similar variation of *i, u, e*, for O.E. *ӯ*.[1]

5. O.E. palatal *c* remains in the North as *c(k)*, but becomes *ch* in the Midland and the South; *wercheth* 334; *worchest* 835; *iche* 451; *uche* 2117; *lich* 483, 754, 895, etc.; *swich* 855, 2010; *such* 2054, 2098; *michel* 968; *muchel* 2135; *quench* 996; *wrecches* 1139; *eche* 1679. Exceptions are frequent: *þenke* 831, 891; *ek* 885; *lyk* 639, 894, 1669; *wirkeþ* 789; *mikel* 2157; *ilke* 2175, 2233.

6. O.E *hw* becomes *hu(qu)* in the North, *wh* or *w* in the Midland, and *w* in the South: *whan* 11, 75, etc.; *who* 104; *what* 126, 218, etc.; *where* 142, 249, etc.; *whi* 1831, etc.; *whil(e)* 295, 1066, etc.; *whom* 413, 1128. Forms with *w* only are fairly frequent: *wich* 111, 1902, 2112; *woso* 161; *weþer* 675, 678; *wan(ne)* 820, 1758; *war* (whether) 1749; *wil* 1809; *wal* 1731. An inorganic *h* is added in *while* 2110. The pronoun *who* in its various forms usually appears without *w*[2]: *hos* 92; *hoso* 147, 345; *hose* 311, 1034; *ho* 1029.

7. The personal endings of the present indicative are definitely Midland: in the singular 1, -*e*; 2, -*est*, -*st*; 3, -*eth*, -*th*; in the plural -*e*, -*en*, -*on*.

(1) *make* 3; *speke* 125; *have* 267; *sey* 300; *se* 425, etc. *Haþ*

---

[1] See Morsbach, *Über den Ursprung der Neuenglischen Schriftsprache*, Heilbronn, 1888, p. 38 f. and p. 41 f. For similar conditions in later documents see Lekebusch, *Die Londoner Urkundensprache von 1430–1500*, Halle, 1906, p. 13 f.

[2] See Kaluza, *Gram.*, p. 80, § 256 b.

in 810 takes its form from the relative *that* rather than from its antecedent, *I*.

(2) *shynest* 5; *lenest* 6; *hast* 8, 26, etc.; *gost* 99, 433; *stoppest* 241. In a few instances where the verb is followed directly by the personal pronoun or by a word beginning with a þ, the final *t* has been dropped: *comes þou* 398; *has þou* 697, 767 (see *hastou* 1157). In one place *-es* is demanded by the rime, though *-est* is written: *rydest* : *sydes* 1593. This, being a unique case, is probably an indication of false accord due to the necessities of rime, rather than of the author's dialect.

(3) *crieth* 31; *hath* 35, 88, etc.; *hauep* 539, 982; *souketh* 32, 124; *shyneth* 80; *doth* 166, 226; *cometh* 389, etc. The following forms are irregular: *haht* 42; *fedeht* 45; *passet* 158; *taket* 787; *witnesset* 1939; *suffred* 319; *drynged* 650. The irregularities in these cases are probably to be explained as the results of scribal carelessness, not as examples of dialectical variations. Three instances of the Northern ending occur: *has* 102, *failes*, riming with *nailes*, 884, and *sais*, 122. Evidence in regard to the author's usage based on this rime would be offset by the rime *deth* : *slep* in 823-4 and 1369-70. Southern and south Midland forms in contract verbs occasionally appear:[1] *stant* 1380, 1386; *stand* 1762; *set* 1664; *bynt* 1224; *lyþ* 1017; *ȝelt* 1798; *shent* 481.

(4) Plural forms: *blesse* 25; *drynke* 275; *loue* 305; *bynde* 413; *louon* 404; *sitton* 407; *maken* 476; *clepon* 543; *don* 1723. *Han* 202, 329, 455, etc., is the regular form, but *haue* is also found (see 2199, 2213, 2218). Both *ben* and *arn* are used, but *ben* the more frequently (*ben* 116, 119, 340, 417, etc.; *arn* 75, 333, 388, etc.). There is only one instance of a plural in *-eth* : *trauayleþ* 335, which is probably influenced by the preceding relative þ*at* or by the following imperative plural, *loketh*. The consistent use of *-e, -en* in the plural leaves no doubt that the dialect is Midland.

8. The infinitive appears both with and without final *n*. In rimes the *n* is usually dropped: *here* 7; *grete* 11; *loute* 76; *rore* 518; *spille* 534; *folde* 645; *wypstonde* 718; *bee* 282, etc. With the one exception *gropon* 2062, only the monosyllabic infinitives, *don*(e) 1494, 1867; *gon* 295, 1722; and *sene* 763, 893, etc., appear in rime with the final *n* retained. Within the line, however, the infinitive is used as frequently with *n* as without it: *ben* 4, etc.;

---

[1] See Kaluza, *Gram.*, p. 172, § 338.

prayson 8; *tellon* 83; *han* 137, etc.; *dion* 1152; *lion* 1162, etc.; beside forms without *n*; *prayse* 11; *feste* 34; *wexe* 39; *haue* 338, etc.; *fele* 362. In retaining the *n* of the infinitive in so many cases, the dialect of this MS. shows closer relation to the South and south Midland than to the North, where the *n* was dropped early.

9. Past participles of strong verbs usually retain the final *n*. The participles retaining *n* in rime, as in the case of infinitives, are as a rule monosyllables: *sene* 15, 311, 342, etc.; *born* 25, 142, 320, etc.; (*y-, a-, by-*) *gon(e)* 97, 178, 575, etc.; (*y-*) *don* 532, 915; (*y-*) *lorn* 551, 564, etc.; within the line, *born* 78, 321; *taken* 88; *bondon* 406; *fonden* 100; *slayn* 137, 280, etc.; *comon* 143; *seyn* 184; *fallon* 289; *smyton* 459, etc. Participles without *n* in rime are (*y-*) *drawe* 28, 2098; *gnawe* 214; *bore* 360; (*y-*) *bounde* 433, 813, etc.; *mysdo* 582, 1157; *ydo* 1338, etc. Within the line the only examples in the first five hundred lines are *bounde* 24; *ouercome* 228; *smyte* 462, 470; *bete* 462. This retention of *n* in the past participle is usually cited as a Northern characteristic.[1] One would expect in a MS. of the south Midland dialect a more general dropping of this *n*. The dialect of London, however, again shows a parallel usage. Morsbach[2] gives evidence indicating that while in the earlier London documents the past participle of strong verbs usually ends in *e*, in documents dating from the twenties of the fifteenth century, *en* is the prevalent ending.[3] Our MS., dating from the first half of the fifteenth century, would offer further confirmation of that result, for the south Midland district in general.

10. The O.E. *ge-* prefix of the past participle has been dropped as a general rule, though it still appears (as *i, y,*) in a fairly large number of cases: *wroght* 20; *born* 25, etc.; *cauth* 26; *drawe* 28; *likned* 79, etc.; *taken* 88; *dyght* 107, 183, etc.; *schewed* 142; *comon* 143; *hud* 456; with the prefix: *y-born* 129; *ydrawe* 251; *yslawe* 252; *ytake* 328; *ybounde* 411; *yset* 417; *yquyt* 2110; *yhud* 2164. Occasionally *a* takes the place of *y*: *agon* 178, 2133; *aqueynt* 1949. These forms with the prefix and without the final *n* (in the case of strong verbs), show again that the dialect of this MS. is coloured by the South rather than by the North.

11. In the preterite of strong verbs the vowel of the plural is

---

[1] See Morsbach, *Gram.*, p. 14, No. 19; Kaluza, *Gram.*, p. 13, No. 18, and p. 177.
[2] See Morsbach, *Shriftsprache*, p. 142 f.
[3] See Lekebusch, *op. cit.*, p. 133, who finds (*-e*)*n* the usual ending in the documents of 1430–1500.

commonly distinguished from that of the singular; *gonne* (*on*) 230, 256, 285, 1432 (sing. *gan* 39, 151, etc.); *ronne* (*on*) 635, 1430, 1480 (sing. *ran* 537); *shouon* 1558; *kemon*[1] 140, 535, 1475 (sing. *cam* 60, 61); *beden* 1580 (sing. *bad* 270). The second person sing. of the preterite regularly preserves the vowel of the plural: *gonne* 217 (3rd per. *gan* 39, etc.); *smyte* 358; ʒ*eue* 196, ʒ*ef* 259 (3rd per. ʒ*af* 713); *bere* 682 (3rd per. *bar* 557). In the present tense of preteritive present verbs a similar distinction between vowels of the singular and plural is preserved: sing. *shal* 11, 130, etc.; pl. *shulle* (*shul*, *shullen*) 326, 303, 352, etc.; sing. *wot* 333, 1231, etc.; pl. *wite* 413. *May* on the other hand is used for both singular and plural. This careful distinction of vowels would indicate the southern part of the Midland district. In the North the vowel of the singular served for the plural as well.

12. Present participles have the ending *inge*, with three exceptions: *stynkynd* 1308, *brennend* 1958, and *feldand* 1308, the first a Southern, the second a Midland,[2] and the third, a Northern form.

13. The pronouns are Midland. The feminine singular nominative appears regularly as *sho* 82, 84, 85, 152, etc. The southern *he* appears, perhaps as a scribal error, in 1667, for *sho* has been used in the preceding lines 1661, 1665.[3] The plural nominative is consistently

---

[1] *Kemon* is a somewhat unusual form. This preterite is found occasionally, both singular and plural, in Southern texts, as in *Octavian* (ed. Sarrazin, Heilbronn, 1885), 1636 of the Southern version; in *Ferumbras* (ed. Herrtage, E.E.T.S.e.s. 34), 260, 3130; and in the Midland *Haveloc* (ed. Skeat, E.E.T.S.e.s. 4), 1208. On this form see K. Bülbring, *Geschichte des Ablauts der Starken Zeitwörter inneshalb des Südenglischen*, Strassburg, 1889, pp. 31, 35, 76. In our text *kemon* is the regular plural form and is not influenced, as in some of the examples quoted, by the needs of rime.

[2] Rather an east than a west Midland form; see Morsbach, *Gram.*, p. 15.

[3] In the lines in question the feminine pronouns refer to the soul represented as the spouse of Christ. VV. 1665–6 read:

Sho syngeþ to him a loue-song
And wepeþ also euer among.

Then v. 1667 changes to *he*, which must, however, refer to the singer of the preceding lines: *Syngyng he mot teres lete*. In the following verses (1669–76) the *he* forms are also open to question. The lines are based ultimately on a passage of the *Canticum Canticorum* (II, 4, Vulgate text), *Introduxit me in cellam vinariam* . . ., in which it is the bride (or the soul, as the passage is interpreted) who is led into the wine-cellar of her lover. There is a similar figure in one of Rolle's *Epistles* (ed. by Horstmann, *Richard Rolle*, I, 294 f.) in which Christ, speaking to the souls of the faithful, says, ʒ*e shall be made drunkene with þe freeste wyne in my celer*. One would expect, therefore, that in the *Meditations* in the passage in question, it would be the soul who is to drink of Christ's wine, not Christ of the soul's. In that case the *he* forms in these lines should be feminine. But the context favours the interpretation of the *he* in v. 1669 f. as referring to Christ, and as being, therefore, the regular masculine pronoun.

Introduction

þei, þey 75, 143, 256, 285, etc.; and the dative and accusative, hem 76, 142, 154, 259, etc. Ham, a Southern form,[1] is found once, 2157. Hur(e) is used without exception for the feminine accusative and for the feminine and the plural possessive 320, 322, 1676, 1680, 1874, 1934; þo is both demonstrative pronoun and adjective 283, 602, 865; and þuse is used as demonstrative adjective 1123, 1624.

14. v for f, a Southern, and more particularly a Kentish, trait,[2] appears once, in viole 95.

II. SUMMARY AND SOURCES OF THE *MEDITATIONS*

1. SUMMARY

FOR a narrative treatment of the life and passion of Christ a simple statement of the theme would be almost sufficient indication of the contents. A meditation such as this poem, on the other hand, is not limited in subject-matter nor in method of treatment. It will simplify the later discussion, therefore, to trace, first of all, the general course followed by the poet in his meditations. He has not attempted a formal arrangement for his contemplations, such as the "double meditation" to be made before each of the liturgical hours, which the *Mirrour of St. Edmund*[3] outlines; nor has he divided his material into "days" as Bonaventura[4] does. There is no one guiding thread running throughout the poem. The events which form the subject of the meditations are often introduced out of their chronological order; or, again, some topics, such as the crucifixion, are treated several times in different parts of the poem. At one point the poet will indicate his transition from one subject to the next in so many words:

437-8 : More wolde I speke of þis matere,
But I mot leue of riȝt here.

The pronoun *he* in v. 1667, however, can hardly be read otherwise than as a feminine—either the outcropping of a Southern form, or a scribal error for the form *sho* used elsewhere in the text.

[1] See Diehn, *Die Pronomina in Frühmittelenglischen*, Heidelberg, 1901, p. 21. Morsbach, *Schriftsprache*, pp. 122 and 123, finds *ham* only rarely in the London documents.

[2] See Kaluza, *Gram.*, p. 13; Morsbach, *Gram.*, p. 23.

[3] Printed by Horstmann, *Richard Rolle*, I ; see p. 235 : *Bot nowe for to do þis, þan sall þou wit þat till ilke houre of þe daye es dowbyll medytacyone, ane of his passyone, and anoþer of þe toþer sesone.* Before matins, for instance, one was to meditate upon the time, place, and hour of Christ's birth, and then upon the betrayal.

[4] *Meditationes Vitae Christi*, printed in *Sancti Bonaventurae Opera*, Venetiis, 1756, XII, p. 379 f. See also Nicholas Love's translation of Bonaventura : *The Mirrour of the Blessed Lyf of Jesu Christ*, ed. by L. F. Powell, Oxford, 1908.

More often no division is marked: one meditation follows upon another without a break. It is difficult for these reasons to give an orderly account of the poem, and one can only attempt to indicate its chief topics, without pursuing the details of the poet's thought.

The first part of the poem is best described as a hymn in praise of the Virgin Mary. In meditating upon the miracle of Christ's birth, the poet dwells especially upon the wonderful sweetness of the Virgin which was of such compelling power that it drew the Lord of the universe down to earth (vv. 13–48). Christ's coming as a prince of peace is contrasted with the warlike approach of a prince of pride (vv. 59–68). Then follows a "likening" of Mary, such as forms the theme of innumerable Latin and English hymns to the Virgin (vv. 91–128). She is the spring of day, a primerole, a roser bearing an unfading rose; and as the summit of praise she is the bride of the *Song of Songs*.

A few lines of narrative, telling of the coming of the Magi (vv. 131–142) serve as transition to the poet's next theme, Mary "with hure swete child pleyinge" (vv. 143–176). He pictures her solacing the infant Jesus with a flower or an apple, or above all with her singing, for the sweetness of which Christ forsook the song of angels. This passage recalls the setting of many songs and carols which contain the suggestion at least of a similar picture.[1]

In the life of Christ, between the birth and the Last Supper, only one event, the raising of Lazarus (vv. 209–252) is noted at any length. The story itself fills but half a dozen lines. The poet makes it the occasion, however, for extolling the overmastering power of Christ's command, "Com out" (vv. 217–252). He exults over the fiend, powerless to resist that cry, and taunts him with the question:

> 241-2 : Whi stoppest þou not, fend, þin ere
> þat þis word entre not þere ?

No passage in the poem is more evidently the poet's own work. It is worth quoting in full:

> 217-252 : þat dede by name þou gonne to calle,
> "Com out, Lazer, what-so by-falle."
> Þanne myght not þe fend of helle
> Lengur make þat saule to dwelle,

---

[1] In E.E.T.S., e.s. 101, see stanza 6 of song 35, p. 26, and stanza 2 of song 69, p. 65. In Love's *Mirrour*, p. 53, there is a similar picture of Mary playing with Jesus. See also Walter Mapes' poem, *De Maria Virgine*, printed by T. Wright, *The Latin Poems of Walter Mapes*, London, 1841, p. 196, v. 189 f.

> So dredful was þat ilke cry
> To þat feloun, oure enemy.
> The kynges trompe blew a blast:
> "Com out," it sede, "be not a-gast."
> Wiþ þat woys þe fend gan quake
> As doth þe lef whan wyndis wake.
> "Com out" is now a wonder soun;
> Hit hath ouercome þat foule feloun,
> And al his carful componye
> For drede þer-of þey gonne crye.
> ȝet is "Com out" a wonder song,
> For it hath broken þe pryson strong,
> Feteres, cheynes, and bondes mo
> Þat wroghton wrecched soules wo.
> "Com out," þat kynges voys so fre
> It maketh þe deuel and deth to fle.
> Sey me now, þou serpent sly,
> Is not "Com out" an asper cry?
> "Com out" is word of bataylc,
> For it gan helle sone to assaile.
> Whi stoppest þou not, fend, þin ere
> Þat þis word entre not þere?
> He þat seyde þat word of mygth
> Shop hym felly to þe fygth,
> For wyth þat word he wan þe feld
> Withouten spere, withouten sheld,
> And brogthe hem out of pryson strong
> Þat weron holden þere with wrong.
> Tel now, tyrant, where is þy myght?
> "Com out" haþ feld hit al with fyght.
> Thy pryson he haþ fro þe y-drawe,
> And þer-to, þef, he haþ þe y-slawe.

In his treatment of the Last Supper (vv. 257–365), the poet in a similar way omits the usual incidents and concentrates his attention upon one particular phase, in this case, on Christ's farewell discourse. The preparations for the supper, the breaking of bread, the prediction of Judas's treachery and of Peter's denial, are passed over in complete silence, while the washing of feet is dismissed in one line.

From this point the Passion becomes the main theme of the poem. It is not the exclusive theme, however. The poet is continually led away to other topics of meditation and has to recall his thoughts, sometimes with an effort, to recount more of "Jesus' hard penaunce." As a result, in making a rough division of this whole section, one may distinguish four separate treatments of the Passion, as follows:

1. vv. 366–1130.
2. vv. 1131–1348.
3. vv. 1349–1700.
4. vv. 1701–2040.

In the beginning of the first account, there is a suggestion at least of chronological order. The agony in Gethsamene (v. 366 f.), the betrayal (v. 389 f.), Peter's denial (v. 441 f.), the trials before Pilate and Herod (v. 491 f.), and the mocking (v. 535 f.), follow in correct order. The events themselves are not related even in their main outlines. They are hardly more than alluded to, and then almost lost to sight in the figurative repetitions and devotional exclamations which the poet builds up around them. For example, the incident of Christ taken captive at the betrayal becomes an address to the bonds (see v. 413 f.), and a prayer to share the same bondage (v. 429 f.). The mocking of Christ is interspersed with a succession of lyrical passages, partly on the instruments of the Passion, partly on the person of Christ, which forms the distinguishing feature of this first meditation on the Passion. First the thorn and the reed are extolled as symbols of kingly power. Then, adopting the imagery of chivalry, the poet describes Christ's breast (v. 657 f.) as a shield emblazoned in white and red, borne in tournament against the fiend. Lastly, in a series of vivid comparisons he exalts the cross as an instrument of salvation and a ladder " lastyng vp tyl heuene." In such passages the poet forgets the Passion and looks upon the crucifixion only as a triumph. In fact, in one place he compares Christ to a Roman victor, who for his conquest should have been crowned not with the thorn but with the " lorer " (see vv. 555–562).

On the other hand the poet sees in Christ the victim as well as the conqueror. He is the prey of Love, long sought and willingly captured (v. 767 f. and v. 795 f.). With characteristic fondness for direct address, the poet calls upon Love to learn who it is that he has brought to death (v. 847 f.). The lines which follow are a eulogy of Christ expressed in a series of likenings and of contrasts. Christ is the unfading flower, the sun of right, the laurel which crowns the " senatoures " for their labours on earth. Each point of His shame and suffering is paralleled by the corresponding honour and joy which it has brought to men :

        965-970 : He drank galle wiþ eysel sour
                To ȝyuon vs wyn and swete sauour ;

> þat song of lyf gan forte grone
> To bryng vs out of michel mone;
> For a rud þat him was ȝoue
> He ȝaf vs a septre of þe reme aboue.

The poet ends with a triumphant hymn in praise of Jesus' name (vv. 1035–1126). He has not forgotten the purpose of these lines of eulogy, for he concludes this part of his reflections, with the comment

> 1127–8: Now, loue, þou knowest a party
> On whom þou kyndest þy maistry.[1]

In passages such as those just described, the poet has amply proved his power of sustained lyric expression. By his repeated exhortations to Love to learn whom he has slain, he binds these separate lyrics together, and gives to the whole passage a certain unity which is often missing in other portions of his meditations.

With this climax of praise, the first meditation on the Passion ends. Turning back to the scene of the crucifixion the poet calls upon Love once more to witness the meekness of Christ under His suffering. He emphasizes the mourning of Nature at the death of Christ (vv. 1143–1148) in distinction to the callousness of men (vv. 1149–1150), and pictures with sympathetic vividness the grief of Mary at the cross (vv. 1173–1216). In a sense this second description, dwelling rather upon the later events of the crucifixion is complementary to the first, and repeats it only in the opening details. Here, as in the earlier account, the incidents themselves are only brushed in passing. The poet takes the death of Christ as the central point of his meditations. Christ is compared to certain Old Testament heroes, who in like manner suffered persecution or death unjustly (vv. 1253–1272). He is Joseph locked in a pit by his jealous brothers (v. 1255 f.); he is the murdered Abel, with this difference, that his blood cries out, not for vengeance, but for mercy on his brother (v. 1259 f.); he is also Job, Maccabeus, and King David (v. 1267 f.). The poet begs that if he may not die with Christ (v. 1289) he may be as one dead to all earthly pleasure. That thought leads him to an elaborate comparison—in this case a borrowed one [2]—between earthly and heavenly love (vv. 1301–1322), at the conclusion of which he prays that his heart may be turned from love of transitory things to contemplate continually the symbols of the Passion.

This reference to the Passion introduces the poet's third treatment

---

[1] See also vv. 901–2, 951–2, 1033–4.   [2] See p. xxviii. below.

of that theme. Continuing the imagery of his prayer, he commands Love to write upon his heart first one and then another of the details of the Passion (v. 1349 f.). Throughout this section (see vv. 1397–1584), in contrast to his treatment elsewhere he keeps the actual scene rather prominently in the foreground. Here, too, the repetition of details and inversion of order are more frequent than in the earlier passages. For instance, after the sorrow of Mary at the cross has been described (vv. 1455–66) Love is asked to tell of the betrayal; then when he has recounted the death of Christ (vv. 1488–92), the poet returns to the trial before Pilate, repeating in new words much of what he has already told. However, at the end of this section the poet returns to a freer use of his method of figurative exposition, and adopting the imagery already familiar to him, describes the crucifixion once more as a battle in which Christ fights against the fiend with no armour but his own body (v. 1585 f.). Upon this follows a passage on the joy of enduring poverty and hardship for Christ (v. 1605 f.). The poet elaborates upon the figure of the heart as the dwelling-place of Christ, and of the soul as His spouse (v. 1637 f.). It is with reluctance that he turns from the contemplation of these joyful scenes to speak again of the Passion (see v. 1689 f.).

The last meditation on the Passion is prefaced by a paraphrase of a complaint of Job, prototype of Christ, against his enemies (vv. 1701–1734). The Passion itself is described in a series of contrasts between the former power of Christ and his present humiliation, the complementary members of the series being introduced each time by the words *yesterday* and *to-day*.[1] The same devices of repetition and contrast are used again (v. 1827 f.) in a long complaint upon Christ's sufferings. Here the poet employs a succession of rhetorical questions beginning with the word *Whi*:

    1831 f: Whi is lyʒt cast into derknesse?
           Whi haþ þe flour lorn his fairnesse?
           Whi shal þe vyne drynkon galle?
           Whi wepeþ þo ye bryʒtest of alle?

---

[1] The suggestion for this contrast of *yesterday* and *to-day* may have come to the poet from such a passage as that in the liturgical office, *Festa Transfigurationis et Nominis Jesu*, where a contrast is drawn between Jesus in the glory of his transfiguration and Jesus in the humility of his manhood, with a similar alternation of *heri* and *hodie*. Part of the passage follows: *Heri celebravimus Jesum in celso montis vertice transfiguratum: hodie in imis terris humiliatum. Heri qualis apud patrem erat Jesus prodebat corporis sui candore: hodie celebramus quomodo latens divinitas operatur nostra sub humili natura sacramenta salutis.* . . . Printed in *Breviarium secundum usum Ecclesie Eboracensis*, II, Col. 768, Surtees Soc. 75, London, 1883.

The poet's complaint and mourning, however, give way to another of his triumphant outbursts as he describes the joy which Christ's presence imparts; martyrs, saints, and fathers are named who bore witness to that fact (vv. 1937-2002).

With his meditations on the Passion ended, the poet recalls briefly a few of the events following the crucifixion: the harrowing of hell (v. 2041 f.); Christ's appearance to Mary Magdalene (v. 2045 f.), and later to Thomas and the other disciples (v. 2059 f.); the ascension, told in one line (v. 2070); and the descent of the Holy Ghost (v. 2071 f.).

The last part of the poem, like the first, is devoted to the Virgin. In a passage on the Assumption (vv. 2075-2118) the poet verges almost upon argument in his desire to show the reasonableness of Mary's bodily incorruption. Then dwelling upon the familiar theme of the frailty of human nature and the transitoriness of human life (v. 2173 f.), he makes a final appeal to Mary for her intercession at the day of doom. He bids her in conclusion open his book before the Lord,

vv. 2245-6 : þat for þis preysyng sake
Somdel he wole oure serwes slake.

As the summary indicates, these meditations are made up partly of material that is conventional both in subject-matter and in phrasing, together with other material that strikes one as fresh and original. The conventional elements offer no clue to the author's definite indebtedness to other works. Such details in the description of Jesus as the "red blood on skin so white," or the "teres running by his lere;" and such imagery as that representing the soul as spouse of Christ, or Mary as the captor of the Unicorn, can be paralleled many times both in English and Latin religious works. A poet writing upon these subjects, and especially one writing as late as the author of the *Meditations*, could hardly avoid the use of such conventional ideas and phrasings. Their appearance in his text indicates nothing more than his general familiarity with literary conventions used in descriptions of the Passion, in expressions of the soul's longing for Christ, and in praisings of Mary. On the other hand certain passages of the *Meditations* show clearly from what definite sources the poet drew a part of his material. Thus, aside from his use of the Bible, he is indebted to Richard Rolle, to Hugo of St. Victor, and to the unknown author of an *Orison of the Passion*. What he owes to each of these will be pointed out in the following pages.

2. The Orison of the Passion

The author of the *Meditations* has incorporated into his text practically the whole of a shorter poem on the same subject, which may be appropriately named from the word applied to it in the introductory rubric, an *Orison of the Passion*. The poet's treatment of this poem is characteristic of his other borrowings also, and may be considered profitably in detail.

The *Orison*, which is printed here for the first time,[1] is a poem of 154 lines written in couplets. It has been preserved in the following MSS., none earlier than the second half of the fourteenth century:

1. MS. Bodley 850 (S.C. 2604).[2] Second half of the fourteenth century. Fol. 90 a–91 b. The text is written as prose; vv. 12, 57–62, and 149 have been omitted.

2. MS. Bodl. e. Mus. 232 (S.C. 3657).[3] Fol. 62 a–65 b. The poem is preceded by the following rubric : *In seiynge of þis orisoun stynteth and bydeth at euery cros and thynketh whate ȝe haue seide. ffor a more deuout prayere ffond I neuer of þe passioun who so wold deuoutly say hit as hit folweth.* Crosses are occasionally set in the margin opposite the successive points of meditation.

3. MS. Bodley Add. E. 4 (S.C. 29110).[4] First half of the fifteenth century. This MS. is a parchment roll, containing an imperfect copy of the *Arms of Christ*, with drawings, and the *Orison*. The text of the latter is rubbed in places. It is preceded by a rubric similar to that in Bodl. e. Mus. 232, and the crosses again are occasionally marked in the margin.

4. Pepys MS. 2125 (Magdalene Coll., Camb.).[5] Fifteenth century. Fol. 76 b. The poem bears the following title used in this MS. only : *Memoriale de ligne crucis.* The text is incomplete, preserving only about seventy lines.

5. Gurney MS.[6] End of the fourteenth century. Fol. 182 b. The introductory rubric is as follows : *Here beginniþ an holy meditaciun. Behofliche to be pouht or seyd with deuociun.*

6. Longleat MS. (1).[7] Fifteenth century. Art. 14.

---

[1] See the Appendix below.
[2] See Carleton Brown, *A Register of Middle English Religious and Didactic Verse*, Oxford, 1916, I, p. 37.
[3] See *Register*, p. 46. The *Orison* is printed from this MS. in the Appendix of the present work.
[4] See F. Madan, *A Summary Cat. of Western MSS. in the Bodleian Library at Oxford*, Oxford, 1905, V, p. 560 f., and *Register*, p. 120.
[5] See *Register*, p. 218 f.
[6] See *Register*, p. 469. I am indebted to Professor Brown for the use of his transcription of the *Orison* from this and from the preceding MS.
[7] See *Register*, p. 473 f. and *Hist. MSS. Com. Report*, London, 1872, III, Appendix, p. 181.

Introduction

7. Longleat MS. (2).[1] Fifteenth century.
8. Lambeth MS. 599.[2] ? Fourteenth century. Fol. 134 a. Only vv. 1–12 are preserved.
9. Brit. Mus. Addit. MS. 39574 (Wheatley MS.).[3] Early fifteenth century. Fol. 1 a–4 b.

The *Orison*, as the rubric suggests, is a devout prayer or meditation based on the Passion. The meditation falls into two parts, distinguished from each other in subject-matter and in form of address. In the first part (vv. 1–74) the poet thinks upon the Passion, tracing its course in very general outline, and appealing to Jesus to write each incident upon his heart.[4] This repetition of the word *Writ* at the beginning of successive quatrains is the distinguishing form of appeal in this part of the *Orison*. In the second part (vv. 75–154), the prayer is a more personal expression of a desire to feel the power of Christ's love (v. 79 f.) and to learn the joy of enduring hardship for His sake (v. 105 f.). The poem closes with an appeal to Jesus for His mercy and for the support of His presence at death (v. 133 f.). In this half of the poem the figurative *Writ on my heart* has been dropped and in its stead the name *Ihesu* is repeated at each new phase of meditation. Between these two parts, however, there is no break, but a progression of thought. The poet's meditation upon the Passion has led him to think upon the love of Jesus, which the Passion exemplified. Such, at least, appears to be the connecting link which the poet meant to suggest by the words of his transitional lines:

> Ihesu, write þus þat y mote know
> How mokel loue to þe y owe.[5]

This, in brief, is the poem which the author of the *Meditations* incorporated into his own work with scarcely an omission and with very few alterations.[6] The fact of his borrowing, however, is not so significant as the method. He has broken up the *Orison* into its component quatrains and octaves,[7] and these fragments he has

---

[1] See *Register*, p. 474 and *Hist. MSS. Com. Report, loc. cit.*
[2] See *Register.* p. 440 f.
[3] The Wheatley MS. is being edited for the E.E.T.S. by Miss Mabel Day, to whom I am indebted for notes on this version of the *Orison*.
[4] The following incidents or phases of the Passion are spoken of: Jesus' friendly greeting to Judas at the betrayal (vv. 9–20); Jesus taken captive and led before Pilate (vv. 21–24); the Jews' demand for his crucifixion (vv. 25–28); the shame of Jesus before his enemies (vv. 29–32); the bearing of the cross (vv. 33–40); the crucifixion (vv. 41–52); Mary's grief (vv. 53–60); a prayer on the instruments of the Passion (vv. 61–74).
[5] MS. Bodl. Add. E. 4., vv. 75–6; see the Appendix.
[6] The first four verses and vv. 19–20 are the only lines omitted.
[7] Twice a group of fourteen verses is left intact (vv. 61–74, 141–154) and once one of twelve verses (vv. 113–124).

scattered over the whole extent of his own poem. The first borrowing, for instance, appears at v. 399 f; the last, at v. 2027 f.[1] The excerpts are usually widely separated from each other, so that their common relationship as parts of the same poem is completely obscured. It is only because the lines have been adopted almost without alteration that, with the *Orison* at hand, their source in that poem can be recognized unmistakably.

In two places the process of shifting has resulted in a curious reuniting of passages from the *Orison*. Verses 1609–1640 of the *Meditations*, for instance, are made up of the following lines from the shorter poem: 113–124 + an original quatrain + 105–112 + 125–132. In spite of the evident reversal of their original order, the lines do not read disconnectedly, because of the fact that they are taken from a part of the *Orison*—the passage on the joy of suffering hardship for Christ—in which there is no strict sequence of thought to be preserved. In the second passage reconstructed from the *Orison*, the result is not so satisfactory. The lines in question, vv. 1331–1378, correspond to the following groups from the *Orison*: 91–94 + 61–74 + 53–56 + an original couplet + 5–8 + 41–48 + an original quatrain + 9–12 + 21–24. Here the borrowed lines are from the section of the *Orison* in which the Passion is outlined and the shifting of their order in the *Meditations*, consequently, destroys the proper sequence of events. One finds, for instance, the betrayal (vv. 9–12, or 1371–74 of the *Meditations*), coming after the description of the crucifixion (vv. 41–48, or 1359–66 of the *Meditations*). Such a reversal of incidents, as the summary of that poem has shown, is characteristic of other parts of the *Meditations*. The trait stands out the more clearly here where the author has achieved disorder even at the expense of disarranging a fairly well-ordered text.

The lines on the Passion taken from the *Orison* are used to introduce the third description of that subject in the *Meditations*. They are a mere fragment in the longer text, but they seem to have set the pattern for the author's method of treatment throughout this section. He has adopted the formula, *Writ*, and he has carried out the division into quatrains (see v. 1431 f.) in many of the verses in this portion of his poem. It is a method which would lend itself easily to the author's habit of repetition; and in fact, one finds him here returning again and again to the same phase of the Passion. Thus several quatrains in different parts of this passage describe the indignities

---

[1] The corresponding passages in the *Orison* and the *Meditations* are indicated in the numbering of the text of the *Orison*; see the Appendix.

offered to Jesus before the crucifixion (see v. 1367 f.; 1391 f.; 1511 f.). Moreover, the repetition of one word in successive lines is entirely in keeping with the author's practice. One need only point to the passage on *Com out* (v. 218 f.), and to the still more striking repetition of *Why* in vv. 1827-71. It is not difficult to see, therefore, why the method used in the *Orison* would prove attractive to the author of the *Meditations*. He does not abandon it altogether with this section of his poem, but in the fourth account of the Passion he occasionally introduces a new phase of his meditation with the familiar *Writ* (see vv. 1702, 1735, 1743, 1803, 1811).

In adopting the *Orison's* formula of appeal, however, the author of the *Meditations* has made one noteworthy alteration. He has substituted *Love* in place of *Jesus* as the person addressed. The change appears with the first use of the *Writ* formula in vv. 1349-50 (*Orison* vv. 53-54):

> Loue þat art so mykel of myȝt,
> Writ in myn herte þat reuful syȝt.

The change is carried through consistently wherever this form of appeal is used.[1] The personification of Love is a characteristic device in the *Meditations*. In the first meditation on the Passion, it may be remembered, Love was called upon repeatedly to witness what victim he had slain. The change made in the lines from the *Orison*, therefore, is in perfect accord with this earlier usage, and reveals the author's hand at work in the midst of his otherwise almost literal borrowing. It is indicative, too, of the direction of the borrowing, that it is the author of the *Meditations* who is the reviser, and not the author of the *Orison*. For the direct appeal to Jesus in the latter poem, is the more natural, and, as it were, the more primitive, form of address. With the substitution of Love as the power addressed, a more complex and a more artificial conception is introduced into the author's meditations and into his expression of devotion. This elaborate figure is in accord with the preference for personification and for the use of figurative language which appears throughout the *Meditations*.

3. RICHARD ROLLE

THE same literalness which marked the poet's adaptation of the *Orison* to his own poem, characterizes his borrowings from Richard

---

[1] The change of person addressed applies only to the *Writ* passages of the *Orison*, not to the second part. Here the *Meditations* preserves the direct address to Jesus.

Rolle. Definite indebtedness to Rolle is apparent in only three passages. The most noteworthy borrowing is an excerpt from the *Incendium Amoris*.[1] Rolle, comparing the nature and rewards of the love of Christ and the love of the world, describes the world—to be understood as worldly love—by means of a series of vivid antitheses. This passage the author of the *Meditations* translated and inserted into his own poem as part of an appeal to be weaned from worldly desires. In spite of some freedom in translation and general disarrangement of the order of his source—a characteristic procedure—the dependence of the English upon the Latin is not to be doubted:

Incendium, p. 259 f.

Habet enim mundus mendax delicias miseriarum, diuicias uanitatum, blandimenta uulnerancia, delectamenta pestifera, felicitatem falsam, uoluptatem insanam; dileccionem amentem odibilem, tenebrosam, in inicio meridiem, in fine noctem eternam. Habet et sal insulsum, saporem insipidum, decorem deformem; amiciciam horribilem matutinum mulcens, uesperum pungens; mel amaricans, fructum necantem. Habet et rosam fetoris, gaudium lamentacionis, melodiam mesticie, preconium despeccionis, uere nectar mortis, ornatum abhominacionis, ducem seducentem, principem deprimentem. Habet et gementem gemmam, et laudem ludibrium, lilium liuorem, cantum clangorem, speciem, putridinem, discordem concordiam, niuem innigredinem, solacium desolatorium, inopem regnum. Habet et philomenam magis uacca mugientem; merulinam uocem, melum nescientem; ouem uulpinam pellem induentem; et columbam, plus fera furientem.

Fugiamus ergo corporeum immundialemque amorem, cuius dorsum habet aculeum, etsi facies blandiatur; cuius sapor animam secat a Deo, et balneum cremat igne inferorum; cuius aurum in cinerem uertitur, et thus sulphureum incendium emittet.

Medit., vv. 1303-1324.

þat loue is cleped hate and grame,
Vnsauory salt, preysyng of blame,
Fairnesse of fulthe, fruyt of mornyng,
ffayr spryng of day and foul euenyng,
Bytter hony and swete poyson,
Stynkynd rose, feld and pryson,
Serful ioye and wepynge song,
Blod-red lilie and ryʒt of wrong,
Blak snow and loue of discord,
Pore richesse and bonde-lord,
Sobrenesse boþ wilde and wod,
Bernynge baþ and harmful god,
A turtil clad in a wolues skyn,
A culver of þe lyons kyn,
A nyʒtyngale wiþ an oxes þrote,
A þrostel with an asse note,
A flour wiþ galle al by-gon,
Encense y-mad al of brymston,
Blynd fir gurd wiþ derknesse
þat haþ brennyng and no lyʒtnesse.
Nou, herte, let þuse loues gon
And set þy loue on Cryst alon.

[1] Edited by Margaret Deanesly, *The Incendium Amoris of Richard Rolle of Hampole*, University of Manchester Publications, XOVII, Manchester, 1915.

In most cases the corresponding Latin and English phrases can easily be matched. Occasionally the translator has abandoned the exact contrast given in the Latin, and has evolved a comparison of his own, as in *blod-red lilie* (v. 1310) for *Lilium liuorem* (p. 259), and *bondelord* (v. 1312) for *principem deprimentem* (p. 259). In translating *ouem uulpinam pellem induentem* (p. 260) by the line, *A turtil clad in a wolues skyn* (v. 1315), he has made a mistake with ludicrous result.[1] The suggestion for his grotesque rendering of Rolle's *merulinam uocem, melum nescientem* (p. 260) by the words, *A prostel with an asse note* (v. 1318), he probably found in Rolle's equally grotesque antithesis immediately preceding: *Habet et philamenam magis uacca mugientem* (p. 259). These inaccuracies, as well as the omissions and disarrangements which the translator has made, are easily explained by the fact that he had a rather complicated passage to turn not merely into English, but into verse as well.[2]

One looks in vain for other indications of direct borrowing from the *Incendium*. The subject-matter of the *Incendium*, which is in part an autobiography, and to a greater extent an exposition of the divine love experienced in the contemplative life,[3] would have little in common with the subject-matter of the *Meditations*. Even where similarities appear, as for instance, in their common conception of love as a force binding the soul to God,[4] or wounding the lover's heart,[5] the resemblances are too vague and the ideas expressed too widespread,[6] to be accepted as proof that in these instances, too, the author of the *Meditations* was using the *Incendium*. Only in the one passage which has just been discussed is the evidence of his indebtedness convincing.

In addition to the *Incendium* Rolle's *Meditatio de Passione*

---

[1] Perhaps he read *auem* for *ouem*, or found it thus written in the MS.
[2] It is interesting to compare this metrical translation with the same passage in the prose translation of the *Incendium*, made by Richard Misyn in 1435, and therefore of the same period as the MS. of the *Meditations*. See *The Fire of Love*, ed. by R. Harvey, E.E.T.S. o.s. 106, p. 89 f. There is no question of relationship between the two. The only correspondences in phrasing (see *bittyr hony*, p. 89 and v. 1307 ; *snaw blakness*, p. 89 and *blak snow*, v. 1311) appear in passages which could hardly have been translated otherwise. Misyn, giving a literal and orderly rendering of the Latin, shows none of the peculiarities of wording noted above.
[3] See Deanesly, *Incendium*, introduction, p. 40 f.
[4] See *Incendium*, pp. 276 f., 255, 257 ; *Meditations*, v. 813.
[5] See *Incendium*, p. 197 ; *Meditations*, v. 434.
[6] For instance in the *Orison* the same conceptions occur; see v. 85 and v. 109 f.

Domini,[1] written in English prose, has furnished the *Meditations* with certain figures of speech. In the *Meditatio*, the body of Jesus, marked with wounds, is described in a series of similes. Two of these, which, as far as I know, are peculiar to Rolle, reappear in the *Meditations* with the same application:

Rolle I, p. 96.	*Medit.*, v. 1467 f.
þanne was þi bodi lijk to heuene; for as heuene is ful of sterris, so is þi bodi ful of woundis . . .	Writ his body with blod y-spreynt As is þe welkene with sterres y-peynt
p. 97.	v. 1469 f.
Swete Ihesu, ȝit þi bodi is lijk to a mede ful of swete flouris & holsum herbis; so is þi bodi ful of woundis, swete saueringe to a deuout soule . . .	Or as is þe medwe in May Byset wiþ many a flour ful gay.

It is obvious that the similes in the *Meditations* are a reproduction, somewhat abbreviated, of Rolle's. The first of them the poet has already used in an earlier passage in the *Meditations* with a slightly different but equally appropriate application, namely, to the body of Jesus covered with bloody sweat in Gethsemane (see vv. 377–78). Possibly a third figure from the same list is to be recognized in the following lines:

Rolle I, p. 97.	*Medit.*, v. 1531 f.
More ȝit, swete Ihesu, þi bodi is lijk a book writen wiþ reed enke: so is þi bodi al writen wiþ rede woundis. Now, swete Ihesu, graunte me grace often to rede upon þis book, and sumwhat to vndirstonde þe swetnes of þat writinge, & to haue likinge in stodious abidinge of þat redinge . . .	Loue, with such noble wrytyng þou makest a bok of gret lykyng. What tyme I rede þat bok a-ryȝt, þanne am I glad, ioyful, and lyȝt . . .

It is not quite clear from the lines in the *Meditations* whether the *bok* is Christ's body, as in Rolle's figure, or a less figuratively conceived parchment. In addition to this ambiguity, one is less sure of the source of this than of the first figures, because the comparison of Christ's body to a book is a widespread convention,[2] and therefore

---

[1] Printed in Horstmann, *Richard Rolle*, I, p. 83 f. and p. 92 f. The references are to the second and fuller version of the *Meditatio*.

[2] It is the figure underlying the conception of Christ's body as the charter of salvation. For examples, see M. C. Spalding, *The Middle English Charters of Christ*, p. xlvi f. See also the following passage from the *Orologium Sapientiæ*, printed by Horstmann, *Anglia*, X, p. 340: *Loo, sone, þees beþe þe firste princyples and techynges þe wheche euerlastynge wisdame* [i.e. Christ the speaker] *giveþ to þe and seche oþer here loveres; þe wheche beþ writene and gravene in þis opune boke as þou seeste, þat is to seye, in mye bodye crucifyede.*

might have been suggested to the author of the *Meditations* from other writings. On the other hand in both Rolle and the *Meditations* special emphasis is placed upon the reading of the book and on the joy of such reading. In the *Meditations* the poet calls it a *bok of gret lykyng;* Rolle speaks of the *swetnes of þat writinge,* and prays *to haue likinge* in studying it. The use of the word *liking* in the *Meditations* in this context may not be a chance resemblance, but an echo from the earlier work. Moreover, since the comparison occurs in the same section of the *Meditations* which contains the other figures taken from Rolle, this one, too, is very probably a reminiscence of his *bok* figure.

With this line of contact established between the *Meditations* and Rolle's work, one looks for other evidence of the latter's influence. But unfortunately such evidence is not forthcoming. Apparently the only definite connection between the two meditations is confined to these figurative passages. Rolle's prose meditation is more orderly, and in the description of Christ's appearance and suffering at the crucifixion more detailed than the *Meditations*. With its direct appeals to Jesus at the beginning of each meditation and its prayers at the conclusion of each, that the petitioner may find profit from the subject of his contemplation, Rolle's work is decidedly more personal and subjective. The latter, on the other hand, has a fuller account of the earlier events of the Passion—of the successive appearances of Jesus before Pilate, for instance. The *Meditations*, then, does not follow Rolle's work as a guide. The reappearance of Rolle's similes in its text, in that case, may perhaps be explained not as a direct borrowing from a MS. at hand, but as a quotation from memory.

Parallels in thought and phrasing between the *Meditations* and Rolle's lyrics can be pointed out in many places, but as one has noted in discussing the *Incendium*, these are of the general sort which establish no definite relationship. The prayer for a wound of love, for instance, which is repeated more than once in Rolle's poems,[1] is found in the *Meditations* also in the following passages :

    434. Wiþ swerd of loue ȝif me a wounde.
    813-14. And mak me go with loue y-bounde
        þat I be neuer hol of þat wounde.

---

[1] See Kühn, *Über die Verfasserschaft der in Horstmanns* Library of Early English Writers, Band I and II—Richard Rolle de Hampole—*enthaltenen lyrischen Gedichte,* Greifwald, 1900, p. 47, where instances of this prayer are listed.

There is nothing in these lines, however, to show that the poet was borrowing this conception from Rolle. He could have found the same idea expressed in other devotional lyrics. Or, again, he could have translated the expression from Latin writings, particularly from those of the mystic writers. Bonaventura, to quote one example, makes the following prayer in the prologue of his *Stimuli Amoris:*[1] *Transfige dulcissime Domini Jesu medullas animae meae, suavissimo ac saluberrimo vulnere amoris tui.* Rolle's lyrics cannot be considered as the actual source of passages of similar content in the *Meditations*. One may conclude, however, with some certainty, that Rolle's lyrics formed part of the literary heritage of the author of the *Meditations*.

4. THE BIBLE.

A few passages in the *Meditations* are translations of parts of the Bible. They are, perhaps, quoted from memory, rather than from the open book, for in no case do the quotations follow their source consecutively. Christ's discourse at the Last Supper (vv. 265-361), for instance, begins with a translation of Luke xxii. 15 :

267-68 : Desired I haue with gret longynge
To ete wiþ ȝow at my wendynge.

After an interruption expressing the sorrow and despair of the disciples at Christ's announcement of his separation from them, the discourse is continued according to the Gospel of John. Scattered verses and parts of verses from the thirteenth to the seventeenth chapters, together with two passages from Matthew, are combined into a single uninterrupted discourse.[2] The poet has consequently ignored

[1] *Sanctae Bonaventurae Opera*, edition cited above, XII, p. 3.
[2] The corresponding passages in the *Meditations* and the Bible are indicated in the following lists :

Medit. :	Vulgate Text :
vv. 267-270	Lu. xxii. 15, 17.
273-276	xxii. 18.
277-290, a passage on the disciples' grief, probably suggested by	John xvi. 6.
295-306	xiv. 2 (last part)-3.
307-310	xiii. 34-35.
311-312	xiv. 21 (first part).
313-314	xv. 15.
315-318	xvi. 33 (last part).
319-326	xvi. 21-22.
327-330	Matt. xxvi. 31.
331-334	John xv. 19.
335-338	Matt. xi. 28-29.
339-344	John xv. 4-5.
345-348	xv. 1-2.
349-352	xvii. 24.
353-356	xvii. 20.

the fact that in the Biblical account part of the discourse was spoken at the Last Supper and part after the company had withdrawn to Mount Olivet. His interest centres wholly upon Christ's words apart from the occasion upon which they were uttered. If this is quotation from memory, it is nevertheless sufficiently accurate, as far as individual verses are concerned, to make clear what particular passages the poet had in mind.

In a similar way the author has selected different passages from the Book of Job, and has combined them into a new complaint of Job (vv. 1711-1732). His translation of the Biblical text is much less close here than in the preceding reconstruction, so that the original fragments are in some cases hardly recognizable.[1] Details, too, are introduced which have no counterpart in the Book of Job.

There is a plausible and interesting explanation for these divergencies from the Biblical text. The persecution of Job by his enemies, which forms the subject-matter of his complaint, has been introduced by the poet as a parallel to the sufferings of Jesus at the hands of his captors.[2] As a result, in certain places the author has adopted phraseology, and added details, which recall conventional descriptions of Christ rather than of Job. The following lines, compared with their Biblical source, will illustrate the point:

Medit., v. 1711 f.
Of my body ȝe make a mark
And shote to me strokes stark.
Blody and bare I stonde stille
And suffre ȝow don with me ȝoure wille.
Stille I stonde and harde I wepe
And alle ȝoure harde strokes kepe.
With harde bondes ȝe han me bounde
And on my body maud many a wounde,
And in my face þat was so whit
ȝe spatton alle with gret dispyt.

Job xvi. 13 (last part)-15.
. . . et posuit me sibi quasi in signum. Circumdedit me lanceis suis, convulneravit lumbos meos, non pepercit, et effudit in terra viscera mea. Concidit me vulnere super vulnus. . . ˙.
xxx. 10. Abominantur me, et longe fugiunt a me, et faciem meam conspuere non verentur.

[1] The corresponding places as nearly as they can be ascertained are as follows:
Medit.:
vv. 1711-1718
1719-1720
1721-1724
1725-1728
1729-1732

Job (Vulgate Text):
xvi. 13 (last part)-15.
xxx. 10 (last part).
ix. 25.
xix. 13, 12.
vi. 12, and vii. 12.

[2] See vv. 1705-6 : For Job þat suffred gret afray
     Bytokeneþ Crist as he wel may.
The poet carries the parallel no further and makes no attempt to "expound" the persecution of Job. This parallel is worked out in detail by Gregory the Great in the *Libri Moralium*, Migne, 75, col. 509 f.

The added details in the *Meditations* which are apparently derived from descriptions of the Passion are particularly the still-standing, the weeping, the hard-binding and the whiteness of face. Other lines in the complaint, however, are close translations of the Latin text, and leave no doubt in the reader's mind that the poet is quoting from Job.[1]

As a third borrowing from the Bible the poet has worked into his description of the Virgin certain details from the *Canticum Canticorum*.[2] Twice within the few lines of this passage he names Holy Writ as his authority, a rare proceeding with this author:

vv. 111–112: þe liknesse of wich speketh Holy Writ
May no man take but men of wyt.
121–122: Milk and hony vnder þi tonge
Hcly Writ sais hit is out-spronge.

There is no reason to question the author's statement. Phrases from the *Canticum*, it is true, are commonplaces in hymns in praise of the Virgin, but the poet was not using such secondary sources. His comparisons are given almost in the full text of the Bible, not in the conventional epithet of the hymn. One finds in hymns, for instance, the expression "tower of David" applied to Mary,[3] from the Biblical phrase *Sicut turris David collum tuum*. . . . (*Cant.*, iv. 4). In the *Meditations* the exact comparison is retained:

v. 117 f: þi faire nekke also þer-wyth
Is lik þe castel of kyng Dauid.

The completeness of his comparison indicates that the poet knew the text of the *Canticum*.

The three passages which have been discussed in the preceding paragraphs are the only ones in which the Biblical material keeps close to the Latin text. It is hardly necessary to point again to the author's characteristic treatment of his source: fairly close translation

---

[1] Cf. *Medit.*, vv. 1721–24:
Curour was þere neuer non
þat myȝte a-wey so faste gon
As don þe dayes of my lyf
þat passen a-wey with wo and stryf.

with Job ix. 25:
Dies mei velociores fuerunt cursore;
fugerunt, et non viderunt bonum.

[2] The passages are as follows:
Medit.:
v. 113
vv. 115–116
117–120
121–123

Cant. Canticorum:
vii. 2 (last part).
iv. 3 (last part).
iv. 4.
iv. 11.

[3] See Dreves, *Analecta Hymnica Medii Aevi*, Leipzig, v. 34, p. 74; *Turris Sion*, and p. 34, *Turris David*; also in a French hymn printed by P. Meyer, *Romania*, xiii. p. 510: *Ave la tur al rey David, ave seinte Mary.*

Introduction xxxiii

of the passages selected, and entire freedom in the recombination of these selections.

5. HUGO OF ST. VICTOR.

The influence of Hugo of St. Victor upon the *Meditations* appears in only one passage, but the evidence of that passage is sufficiently clear to give him a place among the writers known to the author of the poem. The particular work of Hugo's which the poet has certainly read is the treatise, *De Laude Charitatis*.[1] As the title indicates, this work is an exaltation of Love as an irresistible power, at once harsh and beneficent; harsh in compelling its subjects to undergo the severest of trials in its service, and beneficent in leading them in the end to supreme joy. In many parts of the treatise Hugo apostrophizes Love, as for instance, when he expresses his wonder at the supreme example of Love's power, his mastery over Christ. This passage marks the climax of Hugo's praise.

It is a similar presentation of Love which one finds in the *Meditations*. In various parts of the poem the author conceives the Passion as a contest between Christ and Love, in which Love is the conqueror.[2] He, too, like Hugo, addresses Love directly, and expresses wonder at Love's treatment of Christ. In addition to these general resemblances one passage in particular unmistakably echoes the text of Hugo's treatise.

De Laude Ch., col. 974–5.	*Medit.*, vv. 1881–1898.
O Charitas! quantum potes! . . . Si Deus propter hominem tanta pertulit, quid homo propter Deum tolerare recusabit ? . . . Adduxisti illum vinculis tuis alligatum, adduxisti illum sagittis tuis vulneratum. Amplius ut puderet hominem tibi resistere, cum te videret etiam in Deum triumphasse. Vulnerasti impassibilem, ligasti insuperabilem, traxisti incommutabilem, aeternum fecisti mortalem. . . . O Charitas! quanta est victoria tua! unum prius vulnerasti, et per illum omnes postmodum superasti. O charitas! laudavi	Thus was Ihesu wiþ loue take And suffred wo for oure sake, And ȝaf vs ensample also For loue of him to suffre wo. Loue, þou hast bounden þe kyng Þat is lord ouer alle þyng, And send hi. to vs hider adoun To dwelle wiþ vs in oure prisoun. It semeþ þou art more of myȝt Þan is Ihesu þe kyng of ryȝt. To dispute þat wole I not dwelle, Any sortayn þer-of to telle. But þis wot I wel forsoþe, On substaunce þey ben boþe ;

[1] Printed in Migne, 176, col. 969 f.
[2] See vv. 873 f. Loue, whi shapest þou such batayle
    To him þat tok for þe trauayle.
The imagery in the *Meditations* is more vivid than that of Hugo, and the poet emphasizes the ruthlessness of Love as Hugo does not; see vv. 847 f., 861 f., and 1127 f.

xxxiv   *Introduction*

te quantum potui, et multum cogito mecum si quid adhuc sit, quod in laudem tui excellentius possit dici. Nescio enim an forte majus sit te Deum dicere an Deum te superasse. Quod si majus est, etiam hoc libenter et fiducialiter de te dicam : Deus charitas est. . . .

Euon honour and euon blis Boþe þei han, wiþouten mys. For þe bok seyth þat God is loue þat cam adoun fram heuene aboue.

The points of likeness in the two passages are easily seen. It should be noted in the first place, that in Hugo as in the *Meditations*, the part quoted is preceded by a brief summary of the Passion, showing Love's power over Christ. In both writers, Christ's endurance of suffering is held up as an example to men, and in both, Love is victorious. Again, the question of Love's superiority which is raised in the *Meditations* (v. 1889 f.) is implied in Hugo's statement : *Nescio enim an forte majus sit te Deum dicere an Deum te superasse.* There is, also, a suggestion of a similar waiving of discussion on the issue raised (see v. 1892 f.) in the words, *Quod si majus est, etiam hoc . . . dicam.* The answer in Hugo and in the *Meditations* is the same, *Deus est Charitas.* There can be little doubt that in this passage Hugo's work influenced the poet's representation of Love as the conqueror of Christ. Very probably the same influence is at work in other parts of the poem where a similar conception of Love is introduced.

These works, the *Orison*, Richard Rolle's *Incendium Amoris* and *Meditatio*, the Bible, and Hugo of St. Victor's *De Laude Charitatis* represent the sources of the *Meditations* as far as they have been detected. They are not, after all, so important for the material they furnish—for the amount is small in comparison with the whole extent of the poem—as they are for the indication they give of the sort of literary influence which helped to shape the *Meditations*. It is with the mystical writers that the poet of the *Meditations* has the closest affiliations. His poem is admirably representative of the lyric treatment of the life and passion of Christ, a treatment in which the poet, often with a curious mingling of artificiality and simplicity in thought and expression, draws from each incident of his narrative, subject-matter for devout meditation and occasion for the expression of deep personal grief or joy.

Meditations on the Life and Passion of Christ

FROM MS. ADDIT. 11307

[IN printing the text of the *Meditations,* all MS. abbreviations are expanded in italics. Alterations in the MS. reading or additions to the lines are set in brackets. Parts of compound words which are written separately in the MS. are joined in the printed text by hyphens; where the MS. runs separate words together, these are separated in the printed text without comment. The paragraph divisions are those indicated in the MS. Otherwise, punctuation, including with a few exceptions the use of capitals for proper names, has been supplied by the editor.]

Heýl be þou, sone of þe fader aboue,		fol. 7 a. Invocation to Jesus,
Þat man býcome for mannes loue,		
Of þe I make þis praýsýng;		
Graunte it mote ben at þý lýkýng;	4	
And þou, þe sterre þat shýnest brýght,		and to Mary.
To heuene and erthe þou lenest light,		
fforthfulle mýn herte þat I maý here		
To praýson þe þat hast no pere;	8	
Of Dauides kýn maud gentil,		
Þou make mý tonke swete and sotil,		
Whan I þe shal praýse or grete,		
Þat it soune as harpe swete.	12	
Lady, þou were from heuene gret		The Immaculate Conception.
And wyth þe holy gost be-set.		
Þou were with childe as it was sene		
And lýk the lilýe maud ful clene;	16	
Þou conseýuedest al in clennesse,		
Trauaile of býrthe tornd in-to blisse;		
Care of oure kýnde noied þe noght,		
ffor þý child swete al wele haþ wroght.	20	
After þat was a wonder sight		
To se þat lord so mýkel of mýght		
Of a tendre maidons hond		
Ly bounde wýth a cradel-bond.	24	

PASSION OF CHRIST   B

2 Meditations on the Life and Passion of Christ

fol. 7 b.

Mary has captured the Unicorn.

We blesse þe týme þat þou were born,
ffor þou hast cauth the Vnicorn
Þat was so fers in þe olde lawe;
Thorw loue he is fro heuen drawe. 28
Þou hast set him vp-on þý barm
And homlý halsed hým in thin arm.
Kýndelý he crieth after þý tete
And souketh þi mýlk þat is so swete. 32
Now is þis a wonder thýng,
Thus to feste so noble a kýng.
Vessel of seluer hath he non at mete,
His cuppe is a maidons tete. 36
Þat tete was ful of swete lýcour
Þat fedde so þat swete flour,
Til it gan so to wexe and sprede,
Hit heled oure kýnde fro deueles drede. 40

The sweetness of Mary drew Jesus down to earth.

A, maide, mikel is þi swetnesse;
Thi mulk haht banned oure bitternesse.
Hit is fer more dilicýous
Þan angeles mete, I preue it thus; 44
For he þat fedeht angeles alle
Cam doun from þat hie halle;
In thi barm he tok his reste
And seek mýlk of thý blessed breste; 48

fol. 9 a.

Christ, Lord of the Universe,

He þat is so mýkel of mýght,
Þat made bothe þe daý and þe nýght,
Heuene and erthe, sonne and see,
Mone and sterres, as 3e maý se, 52
He sette also the planetes seuene
Vp in þe firmament of heuene,
Euere ilk in his owne spere
For to meue on his manere; 56
He worcheth wederes at his wýlle,
For he maý bothe saue and spýlle.
But bý-leue we maý haue
He cam not to spille but to saue; 60

came to earth without princely pomp.

For he cam not on stedes proude,
With hidous crý ne with trompes loude,
Wiþ sheldes, pauýes, ne wýþ targe,
Wiþ plates, helmes brode and large, 64

Wiþ sharpe swerdes ne w*ith* lang spere,
Ne wiþ non other grisly gere,
W*ith* no pride ne w*ith* no pres,
But mekely as a prynce of pees. 68
Loue, þou art ful mykel of mygth,
Þe may no thyng wiþstonde in fygth.
The mygtful kyng þat is aboue,
He is discomfited thorw myʒt of loue. 72
We pray þe, loue, ententiuely   fol. 9 b.
Of oure hertes þou haue maystry.
Whan þei arn sterne, styf, and stoute,
Thorw þi myʒt make hem to loute, 76
And tenderly to loue þat child
Þat was born of þat maydon myld.
Þat maide is likned to þe spryng of day   A praising
And to þe sonne þat shyneth ay; 80   of Mary.
Pereles, precious of pris,
Sho is likned wel to paradys;
And more I may tellen þerto,
Sho is lik þe firmament also; 84
ffor sho stereþ at wylle, y-wys,
Þe hie sone of riʒtfulnes
Now to hure barm, now til hure brest.
Thus heuene in erthe haþ taken his rest; 88
And now is þis a wonder steuene,
Heuene is in erthe *and* erthe in heuene.
Damesel, þou berest þat flour
Thorw hos fairnesse *and* hos flauour 92
The world þat was welked for elde,
fflorscheþ aʒeyn as flour in felde.
Thow, clene mayde wiþoute viole,
Art likned to þe premerole. 96
Whan floures weron welked *and* al y-gone,
Lyk prymerole þou sprang alone.
Maidon, þou gost with a gerlond   fol. 11 a.
Such was neuer fondon in no lond. 100
Hit is as þe lilye dilicyous;
Hit has no pere so precious.
In þi bosme þat lilie sprang;
Who tok it fro þe, he dede þe wrang. 104

Now is þi bosom a fair roser,
Þere springeþ þe rose þat is so cler.
Þer-of þou hast a garlond dýght
To kýng of kýnges, to lord of mýght; 108
Þat garlond is of roses made
Þat [n]euere shulon falwon ne neuere fade.

Holy Writ describes her beauty.
Þe liknesse of wich speketh Holý Writ
Maý no man take but men of wýt. 112
Hit likneþ þi wombe to a mowe of corn,
ffor bred of lýf þer-of was born.
Þi rodý chekes so semely seet
Ben likned to þe pomegarnet. 116
Þi faire nekke also þer-wýth
Is lik þe castel of kýng Dauid;
Þer-inne ben speres for þe bataile,
Ʒif aný enemý hit wolde asaile. 120
Milk and honý under þi tonge
Holý Writ sais hit is outspronge.
Þi clothes ful of encense swete;
Bred of lýf souketh of þi tete. 124

fol. 11 b.
No tongue can praise her fully.
But though I speke wiþ angeles tonge,
What-so I saide, what-so I songe,
I ne mýgthe neuere, mý ladi fre,
fullý preýson thý bounte. 128
Now is þat lord, þat kýng, ý-born
Þat shal saue þat is for-lorn.

The Visitation of the Magi.
Thre kýnges offredon hým presentʒ,
Mirre and gold and frankensentʒ; 132
In tokenýng of þe Trýnýte
Þeý offredon to hým ʒiftes thre.
The kýng Heroud was wroþ *and* wod;
He spilte þe Innocentes blod, 136
ffor he wolde han slaýn þat child
Þat born was of the maidon mýld.
In þe est þere was schewed a sterre;
Þe kýnges thre þat kemon fro ferre 140
Þat brighte sterre wente hem aforn
And schewed hem where þe child was born.

110. MS. *euere*.

Meditations on the Life and Passion of Christ

Whan þei were comon in-to þat place,
Þere þei fondon þe moder of grace,   144   *They find Mary playing with her child.*
And on hure barm þe kẏng of blisse,
Þe brigtho sonne of rẏȝtfulnesse.
Hoso hadde ben þere wel hadde hẏm ben
Þat moþer and maẏdon for to sen   148
With hure swete child pleẏinge;
Non herte maẏ þenke so gret lẏkẏnge.   *fol. 13 a.*
Whan it gan wepe, þat child so swete,
Sho stilled him with mẏlk of tete;   152
Sho clipte hẏm ofte and keste also,
Gret was þe ioẏe be-twene hem to.
Þat ȝonge child whan it gan wepe,
Wiþ song sho lulled him a-slepe;   156
Þat was so swete a melodẏ   *The sweetness of Mary's singing surpasses all other song.*
hẏt passet alle mẏnstralcẏ;
Þe nẏghtẏngale sang also,
Hure wois is hors and noght þer-to.   160
Woso ente[n]deth to hure song
And leueþ þe firste þan doth he wrong.
Nou maẏ þe harpe his stringes slake,
For it maẏ no mẏrthes make   164
To make oure herte lẏkẏng and liȝt,
As song doth of þe burde briȝt.
Song of angels Crist for-sok
And to þe maidons song he tok;   168
ffram heuon he lighte a-doun ful lowe
Of þat song to herkon a throwe.
Ffor ioẏe and blẏsse aẏ as sho song
Teres were medled aẏ among.   172
Whan hure child was at desese
Sho wolde hẏm with an appel plese;
Outher a flour sho wolde hẏm take,
And sho so wolde his wepẏng slake.   176
Glad is that godeman Sẏmeon   *fol. 13 b.*
ffor now is al his serwe a-gon.   *Simeon rejoices in Jesus.*
He sẏ þe light of ioẏe and blis
Þat man maẏ brẏngon [out] of derknes.   180

161. MS. *entedeth.*   180. MS. *and.*

Vp in his arm þe child he lifte
And God he thanked of his gifte.
Redẏ he was to dethe dẏght
Tho he hadde seẏn þat lord of light. 184
ffruẏt gan to rẏpe vnder þe lef,

Early miracles of Jesus.
Vnder þe moder þe child him thref.
Whan he was woxen in elde
Werkes he wrouȝte feȳȝ *and* selde; 188
ffor at the feste þer he was set,
Pottes wiþ water forþ weron fet.
He tornde þe water in-to god wẏn;
Of grape was þer non more fẏn. 192

The Baptism.
Þou dreiedest þe flod of Noe,
Þou waschest water and water not þe;
ffor whan þou were cristened þer-inne,
Þou ȝeue it mẏght to clense of sẏnne. 196
Onlich þe water of þat welle
Quenchon maẏ the fir of helle.

The Temptation.
Thou were led in-to wildirnesse,
Tempted thorw deueles wẏkednesse. 200
Thow wiþstode, þanne fleẏ þat fo;
Ensample we han to don also:

fol. 15 a.
Wiþ god ensample and god techẏng
Þe peple is lad to lif lastẏng 204
Þou helest alle maner euel
And out of summe þou drẏuest þe deuel.
Thousindes þou feddest wiþ loues fẏue;
The dede þou reisedest fram deth to lẏue: 208

The raising of Lazarus.
Þou reisedest Maudeleẏnes brother
To lyue, and also manẏ another.
He laẏ in g[r]a[u]e daẏes foure;
Þe ferþe daẏ he smelled soure, 212
ffor after dede mannes lawe
His bodẏ was with wormẏs gnawe;
ffor flesch is not but wormes ware
Whan it lith ded and biried bare. 216
Þat dede bẏ name þou gonne to calle,

"Com out" brings terror to the fiend.
"Com out, Laȝer, what-so bẏ-falle."

211. MS. *game.*

Þanne myght not þe fend of helle
Lengur make þat saule to dwelle,   220
So dredful was þat ilke crý
To þat feloun, oure enemý.
The kýnges trompe blew a blast:
"Com out," it seide, "be not a-gast."   224
Wiþ͏̔ þat, woýs þe fend gan quake
As doth þe lef whan wýndis wake.
"Com out" is now a wonder soun;
Hit hath ouercome þat foule feloun   228
And al his carful compenýe;   fol. 15 b.
ffor drede þer-of þeý gonne crýe.
Ʒet is "Com ou[t]" a wonder song,
ffor it hath broken þe prýson strong,   232
ffeteres, cheýnes, and bondes mo
Þat wroghton wrecched soules wo.
"Com out," þat kýnges voýs so fre
It maketh þe deuel and deth to fle.   236   It puts death
Seý me now, þou serpent slý,   and the devil
Is not "Com out" an asper crý?   to flight.
"Com out" is word of bataýle,
ffor it gan helle sone to assaile.   240
Whi stoppest þou not, fend, þin ere
Þat þis word entre not þere?
He þat seýde þat word of mýgth
Shop hým fellý to þe fýgth,   244
ffor wýth þat word he wan þe feld
Withouten spere, withouten sheld,
And brogthe hem out of prýson strong
Þat weron holden þere with wrong.   248
Tel now, týrant, where is þý mýght?
"Com out" haþ feld hit al with fýght.
Thý prýson he haþ fro þe ý-drawe,
And þer-to, þef, he haþ þe y-slawe.   252
After þis discomfiture   The en'ry
The peple com hým to honure,   into Jeru-
                                                      salem.
With palmes and with floures swete,   fol. 17 a.
Wepýnge for ioýe þei gonnen þe mete.   256

231. MS. oud.

8 *Meditations on the Life and Passion of Christ*

The Last Supper.

Þou madest a feste, prynce of prys,
That passeth alle maner delys;
Þin owne body þou ȝef hem alle
Þat eton þanne wiþ þe in halle.　　　　　　　260
Loue þat hadde of þe maystrye
Maude þe make þat mangerye
And alle þo þat with þe ete
Also weron fed with loue swete.　　　　　　264
Þou seydest þanne on swete manere
To hem þat weron þe lef and dere:
"Desired I haue with gret longynge
To ete wiþ ȝow at my wendynge."　　　　　　268
A coupe þou toke with-inne a prowe
And bad hem drinke alle on rowe.

Jesus' farewell to his disciples.

Whan he hadde don also,
Þou spak a word þat wroghte hem wo:　　　　272
"Children, ȝe shal neuere more
Sen me drynkon ȝow be-fore,
Til þat we drynke to-gyderes alle
In heuene in my faderes halle."　　　　　　276

The disciples' sorrow.

Þer was mornyng, weping, and mone;
Alas, how sholde we lyue a-lone.
Þou shalt now parten vs fro,
Lete vs be slayn and gon also.　　　　　　280

fol. 17 b.

Was neuer tempest so gret on see
Þat made shipmen so carful bee,
As þi word made alle þo
Þat þou toke of þi leue to go.　　　　　　　284
ffor þanne þey gonnen þenke anon
How fair þou were of flesch and bon,
Swete in speche, corteys and fre,
And slayn þei wolde ha ben for þe.　　　　288
Þei sholden for soþe han fallon to grounde
As maymed men wiþ dedes wounde

Jesus' words of comfort to his disciples.

But comfort of þi swete speche.
In þat siknesse þou was hure leche;　　　　292
For þou dedest hem mukel disport
With a word of gret comfort;
A while þou seidest þou most gon

And comen aȝeẏn riȝt sone anon; 296
"ffor sothe riȝt as I ȝou telle,
Euere more with ȝou to dwelle.
Suffreþ now a litel while,
ffor I ȝou seẏ withouten ghẏle, 300
I shal gon diȝte ȝou a place
Of gret comfort and gret solace,
And þere [ȝe] shul dwellon with me
And fro me neuer more departed be. 304
As ȝe me loue beþ glad and blẏthe;
I go and come aȝen ful swẏthe.
I make ȝow þis comaundement, fol. 19 a.
Þat ilke loue other with god entent; 308 "Love one another."
And per-bẏ shullon men wel I-se
Mi trewe disciples þat ȝe be.
Hose kepeth mẏn hestes, þanne it is sene
Þat he me loueþ with herte clene. 312
Now wil I ȝow not seruantȝ calle,
But I ȝow clepe mẏ frendes alle.
Þe wordle shal tene ȝou swẏde sore
Wiþ harde happes lasse and more; 316
But loketh ȝoure hope be stẏdefast, "Keep your hope steadfast."
For I haue þe wordle a-doun cast.
Þe moþer suffre[þ] wel to-forn
Serewe er hure child be born; 320
Whon it is born sho feleþ lisse,
Hure bale is tornd in-to blisse;
And þanne þenkeþ sho neuer more
Of wo þat sho felte bẏ-fore. 324
Ȝe [shul] be in place dwellẏng with me
Þere ȝe shulle neuer of serwe se.
This nẏght ȝe shulle for sorwe quake
Whanne ȝe shul se mẏ bodẏ ẏ-take; 328
ffor prophetes han writon of me,
"Whan þe herde is hent þe sheþ shul fle."

303-4. These two lines are reversed in the MS. ȝe not in MS.
319. MS. suffred.
325. MS. han.
328-9. Written in margin, with place for insertion marked.

10   *Meditations on the Life and Passion of Christ*

  Þe world sholde loue boþe ȝow and me
  And we weron of his meyne; 332
  But for he wot we arn not so,
  He wercheth euere sorwe and wo.
fol. 19 b. Ȝe þat trauaȳleþ, loketh to me,
  ffor I shal ȝoure comfort be: 336
  Lerneþ of me now meknesse
  And ȝe shulle haue ȝoure part of blisse.
"I am the True Vine." fforsothe I am a veraȳ vȳne
  And ȝe ben alle braunches mȳne. 340
  Dwelleþ with me as braunches clene
  And þanne shal ȝoure fruȳt be sene.
  Spring a-brod in-to ilk a contre
  Ȝoure swete fruȳt þat þei mow se. 344
  Of mȳ vȳne ho-so is traille
  Of fruȳt maȳ he neuer faille.
  Mȳ fader of heuene pu[r]geþ it so,
  Þe fruȳt encreseþ euere mo. 348
Jesus prays to the Father for his disciples. ffor soþe, fader, now I þe telle,
  I wole mȳ seruantȝ with me dwelle
  In mȳ realme þere I shal be,
  And þei shullen mȳ blisse se. 352
  I praȳ þe onlȳ not for hem,
  But also for alle criston men
  That shullon her-after þorw hure lore
  Leuon on me *and* louon me more." 356
  With þuse wordes and other mo,
  Ihesu, þou smȳte hure hertes so
  Þat þeȳ bȳgonnon to sȳke sore
  And weȳle þe daȳ þat þ[ei] were bore. 360
fol. 21 a. The poet prays for a share in the disciples' sorrow. Ihesu, sende in mȳn herte also
  Grace to fele of þat wo;
  ffor þat maner of mornȳng
  Passeth alle wordles lȳkȳng. 364
  Tho Ihesu wisch þe aposteles fet;
  And on þe mount of Olȳuet
  Whan þou madest þi preiere
The bloody sweat. Þou swattest blod with carful chere. 368

  347. MS. *pugeþ*. 360. MS. *þou*.

A welle of blod sprang out of flesch;
Þer-inne is died a flour ful fresch.
Þe flour so swete þat þet haþ shent
Is diȝt in blod in strong turment. 372
Þe sharpe swerd of erthely loue
Haþ mad þi body blody a-boue.
Strengthe of loue þat is so feer
Haþ mad þy body a red roser. 376
With dropes of blod þi body is diȝt
As þe firmament wiþ sterres liȝt.
Of þe, Ihesu, lene me þi liȝt
Whanne I shal drawe to dethes myȝt. 380
Whanne þou were in þis carful cas   *Jesus is*
An angel made þe solas.   *comforted by an angel.*
Now is þis a wonder sort
Hou maker of mirthe may han comfort; 384
And þou tauȝtest vs þer-by
To praye to þe in oure any,
ffor þou art euere ny at nede,   fol. 21 b.
Comfortynge hem þat arn in drede. 388
Now cometh Iudas, vntrew tretour,   *The Betrayal.*
[H]e neygheþ þe lamb, oure sauyour;
He kisseth þe flour þat shyneth bright,
And vnder hony venym is diȝht. 392
Now was Iudas marchaunt vnwys
To selle þat lord for so lytel pris,
Þat hadde richesse withouten ende
To raunsom with al mankynde. 396
To Iudas, Ihesu, þanne seides þou,
"ffrend, whi comes þou hider now?"
Swete Ihesu, how myȝtest þou so
Clepe þi frend so fel a fo? 400
Sithe þou spekest, lord, so louely
To him þat is þin enemy,
How swete shulon þy speches be
To hem þat hertly louen the. 404
Alas, þou swete prynce of pees,   *Jesus is*
As þef goth bondon gyltles.   *bound as a thief.*

390. MS. be.

12 *Meditations on the Life and Passion of Christ*

    Thi bondes sitton þe ful sore,
    And oure sor is hol perfore.   408
    Þe kyng þat no man myȝte ouercome,
    With loue-bondes he is ẏ-nome.
    Now is oure fader Adam ẏ-bounde,
    Crist goth in bẏtter bondes ẏ-wounde. 412
fol. 23 a. Wite ȝe not, bondes, whom ȝe bẏnde,

Bondɴ, do you not know whom you bind?
    Out of his fẏngres þat ȝe so wẏnde
    Dropes of mirre of swete sauour?
    Whiles he suffred so sterne a shour,   416
    The bondes ben so harde ẏ-set
    Vnder þe naẏles blod hẏm blet.
    The blod comeþ out so gret plente
    That no man maẏ þe naẏles se.   420
    Whan I loke on mẏ sauẏour
    Þat is blod-red as rose-flour,
    I auȝte wel to wepe sore,
    Thouȝ I se of his wo no more.   424
    Verraẏliche whan I þe se
    Gon harde bounden for loue of me,
    Euere I weile þat ilke stounde
    Þat I ne were smẏte with deþes wounde 428

The poet prays to be bound like Jesus.
    Þou þat berest vp-on þẏn hond
    ffor mẏ sinne þat bitter bond,
    With þẏne bondes bẏnd me so
    Þat I wepe þorw þought of þi wo.   432
    Lord, þou gost so faste ẏ-bounde,
    Wiþ swerd of loue ȝif me a wounde,
    Þat mẏn herte þat is hard ful ofte
    Thorw þat wounde wexe softe.   436
    More wolde I speke of þis matere,
    But I mot leue of riȝt here;
    And wiþ þe grace of God bẏ-fore
    I shal speke forþer more.   440
fol. 23 b.   Petre þe apostle folwed ful fere

Peter's denial.
    And neẏghed euer ner and nere,
    Til at þe last drede hẏm tok,
    His owne lord þat he forsok.   444
    He lerned þere thurw þat trespas
    To for-ȝeue in þe same cas

Trespas to hem þat dedon amys,
As God Almyȝty for-ȝaf hym his. 448
Now is þe kyng ful of mercy   *The buffett-*
Brouȝt at abay with hides cry.   *ing of Jesus.*
On cheke and chyn and iche a place
Þei spatton in his faire face. 452
Blynde caytyfs with gret vnryȝt
Hiddon his face þe sonne of syȝt.
Þei han now wroȝt a carful werk,
Hud þe day with nyȝt so derk. 456
His semblaut swete ful of delys,
fflour of loue and lilie of prys,
Is bobbed and smyton wiþ vilenye
Of þat onkynde compenye. 460
Swete cheke, whan I þe se
Smyte and bete for loue of me,
Ruly and red and sore smerte,
Ruþe and wo perseþ myn herte. 464
The cheke þat leneþ angels here liȝt
With strokes delfuly is dyȝt;
ffor shame and for strokes fele   fol. 25 a.
Wexeth red and fer fro hele. 468   *His cheek*
Þe kynges cheke is red for shame   *grows red*
And smyte for synful mannes blame.   *for shame and hard blows.*
Shendshyp and shame greueþ hym more
I-wis þan deden þe strokes sore. 472
Alas, þe lamb þat can no qued
ffor oure shame wexeþ red.
Hys shame and his dyshonour
Maken oure chekes of god colour. 476
A wrangful quest ful of falsnesse   *Right is*
Aȝeynes riȝt bereth fals witnesse;   *overcome by wrong; light*
And so derknesse acuseth lyȝt   *by darkness*
And wrong haþ ouercomen ryȝt; 480
Now shent wermot þe hony-comb;
The wolf haþ maistrye ouer þe lomb;
Þe semblant lich þe lylie clene
Is woxon red wiþ strokes kene; 484
Þe wode wynd þat waketh on water,
Þat maketh shippes to cleue and clater,

14   *Meditations on the Life and Passion of Christ*

        So wod and wilde maẏ not be
        As false Iewes weron þe.   488
        Swete Ihesu, þis stronge fẏght
        Þou suffredest al þis longe nẏght.

Jesus is brought before Pilate, fol. 25 b.
        Aȝeẏn þe daẏ began to sprẏnge
        To-fore Pilat þeẏ gonne him brẏnge.   492
        Thou prince þat hast man excused,
        To-fore þe iuge art now acused.
        Litel þou spak and swẏde softe ;
        Þer-onne Pilate gan wonder ofte.   496
        But þou forthfuldest þe prophecẏe
        Þat was said þorw Ysaẏe :
        Þou art led as lamb to knẏf
        Þat goþ so stille and maketh no strẏf.   500
        Pylat þe iuge parceẏved wel
        Þat it was fals euerẏedel
        Þat þi fon þe beron on honde.

and Herod.
        Bẏ-foron Herodes he dede þe stonde.   504
        Þou stode stille and not ne spake ;
        Heroudes for wratthe gan to quake,
        And in toknẏng of gret dispit
        He dede on þe þo cloþing of whit.   508
        Aȝeyn bi-fore Pilate þou art brouȝt ;
        Þat wikked folk þe louede nouȝt
        Wẏth hẏdous crẏ to crie on þe,

"Crucify him."
        "Do hẏm on þe rode-tre."   512
        Alas, þe folk werse þan wod
        Þat spilton with wrong so riȝtful blod ;
        And Baraban, þat foule feloun,
        Deliueredest out of stron[g] prisoun.   516
        Þe lion whan him hongreþ sore,
        He gẏnneþ for to crẏe and rore ;
        But whan he haþ his preie founde,
        And it falleth to þe grounde,   520
        He hath mercẏ þer-of also blẏue,
        And let it gon awaẏ a-lẏue.

fol. 27 a.
        But þou haddest mercẏ non
        Of him þat stod stille as ston ;   524

        516 MS. *stron*.

But feller þan þe lioun wod
Þou were to spillon þat lombes blod.
Pilat tok him þe at þi wille   *Jesus is delivered to*
To beton hým with scorges grille,   528 *his foes.*
So þat whanne he were bete
Þou woldest him on lýue lete.
But euere was þi crý anon
Til he were on þe rode ý-don.   532
Pilat þanne graunted al ȝoure wille
Þat lord of mercý for to spille.
Þanne kemon ȝe alle him bý-forn   *He is crowned with*
And korendon hým wiþ kene þorn.   536 *thorn.*
The blod ran doun of his face,
fful rulý wax þat rose of grace.
Now hauep Ihesu a chapelet
Of þornes on his heued ý-set.   540
Þe rede blod renneþ bý his cheke ;
Thus ben þe Iewes on hým a-wreke.
Þeý clepon hým kýng and al in scorn,
And corondon hým with sharpe þorn.   544
Now was þat a wonder þýng
So to corone þat noble kýng.
In the kýnges dýademe
Sit þe þorn þat is so breme.   548 *Now thorn is of more*
Now is þe þorn of more powere   *worth than precious*
Þan diamand or saffere.   *stones. fol. 27 b.*
Now haþ perre vertue ý-lorn
And al þe pris [is] in the thorn ;   552
ffor at oure kýnges coronement
Perre is left and thorn is hent.
It was sumtýme þe manere
To ȝýuon corones of lorere   556
To him þat bar him best in fýght
And bere þe pris as most of mýght.
Therfore me þinketh þeý dedon þe wrong—
ffor þou art kýng mýghtý and strong—   560
To corone the with bitter brere :
It sholde han ben of þe lorere.

552 *is* not in MS.

	But wel we maẏ blesse þe þorn,	
The thorn has taken away our sorrow.	For þorw þe þorn oure serwe is lorn.	564
	Þe þorn þat was so sharp and kene,	
	Of serwe it haþ mad vs clene.	
	Min herte þat shal with deth to-breste,	
	It auȝte neuere to hauen reste,	568
	And it louede wel his kẏng,	
	To þenkon on his coronẏng.	
	Þe kẏng to fẏgthe for his meẏne	
	Maketh him an helm of brere-tre.	572
	Reufelẏ his forhed blet,	
	Þat helm on hed so sore is set;	
	His chekes ben al blodẏ bẏ-gon,	
	So sore his helm sit him vpon.	576
fol. 29 a.	Bẏ-hold þi kẏng in his corone	
	And þou shalt for serwe swoune.	
Thorn, why will you not pierce my heart?	Whi ne wilt þou, thorn, mẏn herte perce,	
	Þe peẏne of Crist whan I reherce?	580
	More skẏle it were to do me wo	
	Þan hẏm þat no þing haþ mẏsdo.	
	Þe flour þat is tendre and clene,	
	It nath no gilt to thornes kene.	584
	Whi sholde it þanne with þornes prikke	
	ffelon manẏ a sorẏ prikke?	
	Rede now, hose rede can,	
	In þe forhed of God and man,	588
	Þe lettres he maẏ wel i-wete	
	Weron with sharpe þornes i-write.	
The mocking of Jesus.	Þei setton hem doun vp-on hure kne	
	And seidon, "Kẏng, al heil þou be;"	592
	And was but on hure scornẏng	
	Þat þaẏ clepedon hẏ[m] hure kẏng.	
	ffor shame his hew chaunged anon	
	As doth þe flour whan somer is gon.	596
	Eft þe dedon hẏm shame and shonde,	
	Þei tokon hẏm a reed in honde.	
	"Þẏ septre," þeẏ seidon, "a reed shal be	
	In toknẏng of þẏ dẏgnẏte."	600
	Scornẏng þeẏ smeten hẏm among,	
	Þan siked þo kẏng for peẏnes strong.	

594. MS. *hym.*

Among al his serwe and wo
He ne seide neuere ones, "Whi do ȝe so?" 604
But let hem don with him hure wille, fol. 29 b.
Scorne *and* bete him al hure fulle.
Ihesu, þorw þi septre of shame
Þou broughtest vs alle out of blame. 608
Angels of heuene as wel as we
Ben gẏed with þi septre fre.
Þer-fore, angels, ȝe sholde also
Ȝoure mon make right as I do. 612
Here is a song ful of care,
Þe kẏng is tornd to bysmare.
His herte groneþ þorw serwe *and* grame,
He maẏ not loke vp for shame. 616 Jesus is filled with shame before his tormentors.
Whan þei bi-gonne to leyghe loude
No continaunce þe kẏng þo koude,
So was his herte with shame shent
As lamb with whelpes toþ ẏ-rent. 620
Whan þei seidon þat scornful word,
"Al heil be þou, kẏng and lord,"
His cheke was þanne wiþ red depaẏnt,
ffor shame and shonde he was ful faẏnt; 624
His ẏe þat was so faẏr and bright
ffor shame doun to þe erthe is pẏght;
His tonge is stille *and* speketh no qued, Love makes him meek in suffering.
His herte for shame is wel ner ded. 628
Lo, hou myche loue is of mẏght,
So harde he it haþ in herte pẏght;
He bereth what-so men leẏn him on,
So harde haþ loue his loue ouergon. 632
His swete sẏdes fair and clene fol. 31 a.
I-bete weron wiþ scories kene.
So ronne þe blodes dropes bẏdene
Þo swete skẏn mẏȝte not ben sene. 636
Þanne wiþinne a litel þrawe
ffor peẏne hung his hed ful lawe,
And his bodẏ so lẏlẏe-lẏk
ffor smarte strokes wex *and* sẏk. 640

604 Written in margin.

PASSION OF CHRIST. C

His face wex bliech, his lippes bloo,
Sore to grone gan he þoo.
Þat chaumpioun in þis bataýle
Sore swette for gret trauaýle,   644
As rose be-gýnneþ to falwe and folde
In wýnter for þe frostes colde.

The poet addresses Christ's breast, well of bounty.

Heil be þou, breste, veýne of pite,
fflour of heuene, welle of bounte.   648
Who-so haþ grace of aný þýng,
He drýnge[þ] of þat welle-sprýng.
Brest fel ful of loue fre,
Þou noble trone of charýte,   652
Þou welle flowýng fram heuon a-boue,
Mak me drýnk þorw mýgth of loue.
Brest, in þe is God bý-loke,
How mýgthe þe Ieues on þe ben wroke.   656

It is a shield against God's foes.
fol. 31 b.

Godhede of þe made him a sheld
ffellý to fý3te in þe feld.
Þis sheld is of double colour
Whit and red as rose-flour;   660
Þis sheld is born in tornement
And harde strokes it hath hent.
Whan deþ shal come me to asaýle
Þanne wolde muche þis sheld avaýle.   664
Vnder þi sheld, Lord, þou me couere
ffor dýnt of deþ at fendes oeuere

The poet addresses Christ's heart, conquered by love.

Herte, hou mý3test þou louon so,
Siþþe loue haþ þe to deþe do?   668
But lif þe þinkeþ þou hast ý-founde
Whan þou art ded wiþ loue-wounde;
Or loue haþ mad þe so to raue
Þat þou wenest maistrý to haue   672
Whan þou art slaýn and feld with loue,
Or þou wene to ben at þin a-boue;
Weþer loue þe tau3te to come to lýf
Whan he sleþ þe wiþ his knýf?   676
Wepýng for loue [weþ]er it be wele?
A wounde of loue weþer it be hele?

650. MS. *drynged.*   677. MS. *er*, cf. v. 678.

Ʒe, forsoþe, þis is þe lore
Of loue þat I haue ȝerned ȝore;   680
Thorw mÿȝt of þat lore wis
In strong bataÿle þou bere þe pris.
Þou herte ful of loue gret,
Mi drÿe herte make it wet,   684   He begs a drop of love in his own heart.
And on drope of loue-lÿkÿng
Let me haue of þi welle-sprÿng.
Loue þe made man to be,   fol. 33 a.
Loue þe dede on rode tre,   688
Loue haþ þe ȝiuon deþes wounde,
Loue haþ þe leid ded to grounde.
Þou herte ful of loue fre,
Þe pellican haþ lere[d] of þe   692
His herte-blod to spille and spende,
His briddes mÿschief to amende.
Herte, write wiþ loue-lettre,
Ther maÿ be fonden non þi bettre;   696
Of trewe loue has þou no pere—
I grete þe with mÿ pouere.

Heil be þou, crois, baner of pris,   A praising of the cross.
Poudred wiþ rose and flourdelÿs;   700
In oure werres þou art baner,
Of rose of heuene also roser.
Whan þe fend þe saÿ displaid,
He is ouercome and al dismaÿed.   704
Aȝeÿns þe dar he not fÿȝte,
So dredful art þou to his sÿȝte.
Þe crois is holÿ cherche nest,
Þere maÿ þe turtur brede best,   708
To his paleis þe sparwe fleÿ
Whan crÿst vp in-to heuene steÿ.
Iacob seÿ in verraÿ sweuene
A ladder lastÿng vp tÿl heuene;   712
Þat ledder ȝaf vs a tokenÿnge   fol. 33 b.
Þe crois sholde vs to heuene brÿnge.
Crois, þou art shÿp of Noe
Þat sauest oure kynde wiþ þi tre.   716

686. Written in margin.   692. MS. *lereþ*.

Þou dost þe deuel shame and shonde;
No fo may þi liȝt wyþ-stonde;
Thouȝ þou be he þat fro heuon come
In erthe þou borest þe rede blome; 720
Þou berest þe note wiþ þat cornel
Þat fedeþ al þe wordle so wel.

It bears Mary's fruit upon its branches

A maidon hadde in hure gardẏn
Þe fruẏt of loue þat was so fẏn. 724
Þat fruẏt fro hure þe croẏs fette,
Hie on his branches he it sette.
Þe swerd of þat mẏȝtẏ kẏng
Be wẏþ me at mẏn endẏng, 728
Þat I may fiȝte wiþ help of þe
And make þat foule fend to fle.
Crois, þou art ful of perles clere,
Of lẏȝt is no sterre þẏ pere. 732
In-to mẏn herte sent þi liȝt
And put þer-fro þe derke nẏȝt.
Kẏng of loue wiþ loue to-rent,
Bẏcomeþ it þe wel so to be shent 736
And suffre deþ? forsoþe, naẏ;
But mẏȝt of loue þe maistrieþ aẏ.

fol. 35 a.

Jesus is overmastered by love.

Whẏ wilt þou wiþ loue fẏȝt?
His swerd wiþstonde þou ne mẏȝt. 740
As wẏnter felleþ þe lilie-flour,
So loue þe sleþ þorw strengthe of stour.
Swete Ihesu, þi nobeleẏe
Hou mẏȝt it suffre þe so dẏe, 744
And lete loue on þat maner
Ded to brengon þe on ber?
Or loue be glad with speres wounde
To bere þe þorw and doun to grounde? 748
Loues praẏe I trowe þou be,
So harde he hunteþ þe to sle.

Death and wounds mar his comeliness.

Ȝif deþ ne hadde smẏton þe so
Þat made þi face blak and blo, 752
Þe feld in Maẏ bar neuer flour
Þat hadde be lich to þẏ colour.
In cas þou ne haddest not ẏ-deẏd,
Ho-so hadde þe be þe lilie ẏ-lied 756

Ho sholde no lyknesse han I-knowe
More þan of snow *and* of a crowe.
Þe beaute of þi louely lere
Passeþ alle roses clere.   760
Ry3t as þe flour fair in felde
Passeþ heþen and weykeþ for elde,
fful gret reuthe it was to sene
Þat flesch y-take of maydon clene   764
Wounded wiþ spere, wi*th* scorges bete,
And for loue his lyf to lete.
A swete pray, loue, has þou hent,   fol. 85 b.
Þou hast Ihesu wyth nayles rent.   768 Jesus is the prey of love.
Glad art þou to vnder-fonge
Þe pray þat þou hast sou3t so longe;
Longe þou hast be ful hungry
To hauen þat pray in þi maistry.   772
Now þou etest þat ryche flesch
And drynkes þe wyn of blod so fresch.
Ihesu, loue vpon þe ran
And asked þe to saue man.   776
He fedde him on þe til þou were ded
And paid þe raunsom for man*n*es qued.
Ihesu, þi flesch was medicyne
To man þ*at* was in helle-pyne.   780
Þat flesch was hanged on an hok
And harde nayles, so seþ þe bok.
Ihesu so bri3t as spryng of day,
Swetnesse of þe it lasteþ ay.   784
Strengthe of loue þou au3test knawe
Þ*at* wiþ loue art bro3t so lawe,
Loue now taket a wonder way,
He makeþ þat lyf is deþes pray;   788
He wirketh al ry3t as he wyl,
And what-so he doþ, al it is skyl.
Þan it is ry3t and al resoun
So to do þo kyng a-doun,   792
And þe seruant to make a kyng;
Now is þis a wonder þyng.
Ihesu, þou soffredyst deþ gladly   fol. 87 a.
To wynne oure loue enterly.   796 Jesus suffered to win man's love.

ffor loue þou settest deþ at noȝt,
fful dere þou hast oure loue a-boȝt;
And forte shewe þi loue entier
Þou suffredest deþ on foule maner, 800
fforte make oure hertes colde
Brennýng in loue as we ben holde;
And þat we of loue ne faile,
Þou hiȝtest vs for oure trauaile, 804
What týme we sholden hennes wende,
Þe blisse of heuene withouten ende.
Alas, ȝif I vnkýnde be
And loue noȝt him þat loueþ me, 808
Wath peýne am I wordý be lawe
That haþ Ihesu with loue ý-slawe.

The poet begs that his love-longing may be satisfied.
But þou þat grantest alle grace,
Tak þe in mýn herte a space, 812
And mak me go with loue ý-bounde
Þat I be neuer hol of þat wounde.
Sithen þou comandest me to loue,
Send it to me fram þe a-boue; 816
Siþþe þou art loue and bred of lýf,
Send down a corun to þi caýtýf.
Kýng forthfuld of loue-lýkýng,
Wanne wolt þou stoppe mý longýng? 820
Þou hast of loue so gret plente,
Whý ne wilt þou þer-wiþ feden me?

fol. 37 b.
Hit is worse þan aný [d]eth,
Þis long a-býdýng, for þat me sleþ. 824
Ihesu, of mý lif mak sone an ende,
But þou me sum confort sende.
Kýng of loue, strengest of alle,
I here þe at mý dore calle. 828
Þou fýndest it loke wiþ barres stronge,
But brek hem vp, stond not to longe.

He reproaches love for his cruel treatment of Jesus.
Loue, me þenkeþ þou art vn-wýs
To fede wiþ wermot þe výne of pris; 832
Þou herest hým after drýnkon calle
And ȝeuest him eysel medled wíth galle.

823. MS. þeth.

Ioue, þou worchest alweẏ wrake,
þi loue hou mẏȝt þou forsake? 836
I trowe þat it be þi manere
To brẏnge þin owne frend a-bere.
Þou, hous of euere whit and clene,
Were peẏnted with spotel of Iewes kene. 840
On þi forhed so whit so snow
Thou writest with a thornẏ bow.
The grape þou wasshest in his wẏn,
And an appel of lẏf þat is so fẏn 844
Þou preisest it so harde and sore,
Þe appel of deþ drieþ þer-fore.
Herkon now, loue, ho is þis
Þat þou brengest out of blis. 848

A praising of Jesus: "Harken, love, who he is that thou hast slain."

He is a flour þat welketh nought,
So swete and god to haue in þought.
Al ertheĺẏ blisse I wolde forsake
ffor his loue mẏ deþ to take. 852

fol. 39 a.

He is a flour þat welketh noȝt —
In-to oure hertes wiþ loue-þoȝt —
Or þou be glad swich on to shende
Þat ȝeueth þe lẏf withouten ende. 856
He is so verreẏ sunne of rẏȝt,
His lẏȝt fordoth derknesse of nẏȝt.
Þou liuedest not ȝif he ne were,
ffor sone þou sholdest ben broȝt on bere. 860
Lerne ȝet who þat maẏ be
Þat þou dost blodẏ on þe tre.
Heuene and erthe and alle thẏng
Maẏ not al telle his preẏsẏng. 864
ffor þo þat ben in heuene in fere
Thorw sẏȝt of his loueĺẏ chere

The sight of him rejoices those in heaven.

Ben so fulfilt wiþ ioye and blis
Þei maẏ not wite wath serwe is. 868
As ẏron gloweþ wiþ hete of fẏr,
Rẏȝt so brenneþ hure desẏr,
And þer-wiþ shẏnon so bryȝt
ffor ioẏe of þat semeĺẏ sẏȝt. 872

854 f. No break occurs in the MS., but there is evident confusion in the text at this point.

    Loue, whi shapest þou such batayle
    To him þat tok for þe trauaẏle ?
    He heleþ wiþ his blodẏ wounde,
He has loosed the bond of death. And bond of deþ he haþ vnbounde. 876
    I maẏ him wel þe lorer calle
    Þat crouneþ þe senatoures alle
fol. 39 b. On hẏ in heuene for hure trauaile
    Þat þeẏ haddon in bodelẏ bataẏle. 880
    Of deþes cuppe he dronk a drauȝt
    Þorw which he haþ oure lẏf ẏ-lauȝt.
    He wrot his bodẏ wiþ harde nailes
    To writon vs in bok þat neuere failes. 884
    Boþe wiþ-ẏnne and ek wiþ-oute
    Þat bok was writon wiþ nailes stoute ;
    Þo lettres to þi bon weron set,
    ffor þei sholdon laste þe bet. 888
    But ȝit lesteneþ a litel more :
    Þat lord þat þou tormentedest sore,
    Wiþ herte þenketh on him arẏȝt,
He cleanses the heart. He maketh it lẏch þe lilie brẏȝt ; 892
    Þei it be derk and foul to sene,
    He makeþ it lẏk a paleẏs clene,
    And lich heuene, þat hẏe se,
    Ordeẏned for Godes mageste. 896
    Whan herte haþ þat lord ẏ-hent
    It smelleþ as encense whan it is brent ;
    ffor in him is more swetnesse
    Þan in þe sonne lẏȝt and brẏȝtnesse. 900
    Loue, wolt þou þe soþe wite
    Whom þou hast wiþ woundes smẏte ?
    Þou hast slaẏn þe sonne-lẏȝt,
    Prẏnce of sterres, lord of mẏȝt ; 904
He rules the firmament. He turneþ al þe firmament
    A-boute rẏȝt at his talent,
fol. 41 a. Sonne, mone, and sterres alle ;
    Reẏn on erthe he doþ doun falle. 908
    Whan þis lord feleþ turment,
    Þe sonne-bem with nẏȝt is blent.
    Þou faire body semlẏ and swete,
    Þou mẏȝt onlẏ mẏ bales bete. 912

    891. *Wiþ* miswritten for *wan* or *what ?*

Loue, ȝit I praẏe þat þou wolt here
O þing I mot of þe enquere :
Whan Crist was on þe rode don
And nailes hurte led on vpon his bon,   916
Haddest þou not gret mervaẏle
Whanne þou sẏe þe sonne faile
And at mẏddaẏ les his lẏȝt
And wex derker þan þe nẏȝt ?   920
Whan it wax pale, þat faire face,
Þe nẏȝt be-nam [þ]e daẏ his place ;
Creatures mornedon alle   *All creatures mourned his death.*
Whan colour of þat face gan falle.   924
Alas, loue, whi hast þou no reuthe
Of þat lord so ful of trewthe ?
Þe more þou cast him awaẏ fro þe,
Þe more he preẏseþ þi bounte.   928
Whan þou art fers as a lẏoun,
At þẏ fot he falleþ adoun ;
And him smẏteþ wiþ spere sore,
And he preiseþ þe more and more.   932
Loue, þou mẏȝt noþing blame
Þei I speke of þat kẏnges name.
It is mẏ ioẏe and my lẏkẏng   fol. 41 b.
Aẏ to speke of his preẏsẏng.   936 *It is my joy to praise him.*
He is þe sone of þe fader on hẏ,
Heuenes merthe and melodẏ.
In a cote whit so lilie-sprẏng
A maidon haþ clo[þ]e[d] þat kẏng ;   940
ffor of þat maidon he was born
To ransome man þat was for-lorn.
What eẏleþ þe, loue, þi swerd to drawe   *Why, love, didst thou slay the innocent?*
To brẏnge so swete a child of dawe ?   944
Wilt þou fordon þe kẏng of blis
To spare hem þat han don mẏs ?
The child þat neuere dede harm
Þou takest fro his moder barm ;   948
Þou makest him wepe *and* wo-bẏ-gon
And sparest hem þat han mẏsdon.

922. MS. *de*.   940. MS. *clodeþ*.

Hearken further whom thou hast slain.	ȝet herkene þou, loue, a lýtel stounde,
	And se whom þou hast feld to grounde. 952
	He is a kýng so noble of kýnde
	Þat his bounte haþ non ende;
	He is verraý liȝt þat faileþ noȝt;
	His bounte maý not be bouȝt; 956
	He suffreþ deþ and gret damage
	To quýte vs fro foul seruage;
He wept to give us joy.	He wep to ȝiue vs ioýe and blis;
	He went vs bý-forn þe weý to wis; 960
	ffor drede of deþ he gan to quake
	Strong and stýf vs forto make;
	ffor he was al blod bý-ronne
	Rýche cloþes we han ý-wonne; 964
fol. 43 *a.*	He drank galle wiþ eýsel sour
	To ȝýuon vs wýn and swete sauo*ur*;
	Þat song of lýf gan forte grone
	To brýng vs out of michel mone; 968
	ffor a rud þat him was ȝoue
	He ȝaf vs a septre of þe reme aboue.
Mirth mourns that we may be merry.	Now morneþ mýrþe *and* goþ druý
	To make vs mýrie þat weron soý; 972
	Now welkeþ þe flour so swete *and* dere
	And makeþ vs to florische þat welked were
	The liȝt of daý turneþ to nýȝt
	To make nýȝt cler as is þe daý-lýȝt; 976
	Þe trewe spouse leseþ his lif
	ffor loue of his vntrewe wýf;
	Garlond of þorn þat stak so fast
	Corone vs ȝaf þat eue*re* shal last; 980
	Þe crois þat wroȝte him serwe and wo
	Haueþ oue*r*comen oure felle fo.
Julius Cæsar was not so worthy of the laurel.	Iulius Cesar, þe emperour,
	Ouer-cam neue*r* so strong a stour; 984
	So worþi I wene not he were
	To bere corone of þe lorere
	As þis kýng cam doun fro a-boue
	Þat now is slaýn wiþ swerd of loue. 988
	Þis kýng is charied wiþ þornes kene,
	Bý dropes of blod it is wel sene.

Þe fet þat angeles alle drede
Iewes wiþ nailes on rode gan sprede.   992
ffrom welles of oure sauyour
Spryngeþ water of lyf and swete lycour.
Herte, [d]rynk þer-of þi fulle   fol. 43 b.
And quench þi þurst riȝt at þi wille.   996
Þe face þat was so briȝt of ble
Is now so rewly onne to se.
It waxeth dym, þat eyȝe briȝt,   His eye
And so haue we recouered syȝt;   1000 grows dim,
                                                    to make ours
Þe flour of flesch falleþ away   bright.
And we þat weron welked as hay
And mowe a-doun with sýþe of synne
Aȝeyn to sprynge now bygynne.   1004
Þe nailes in his hondes to
Þe gates of hay to vs vn-do;
Þat swete tonge þat held him stille
Ȝiueþ vs knowyng and speche at wille;   1008
A flour haþ helle-ȝates broke
And let out men þat were for-loke;
Þe kyng him-self is woxen a page   The king
To bryng his seruauntȝ out of seruage;   1012 becomes a
                                                    page to free
Þe sunne goþ a-doun a-nyȝt   his servants.
And so han alle þe sterres lyȝt;
Helþe is syk and sykeþ sore
Þe sike ben woxen hol þer-fore;   1016
Medycyne lyþ ded with wounde,
Comfort and ioye haþ care y-founde.
Ioye and blisse groneþ for wo,
Þe lilye wexeþ blak and blo.   1020
His armes ben drawen out ful wyde,
A sharp spere perced his syde;
Hit perced hastely his herte,   fol. 45 a.
Þat swete syde sore it smerte.   1024
He þat was of þe maydon born,
Whan he was coronet wiþ a þorn,
He wep, for he hadde enchesoun;
Þe blod wiþ teres ran forþ a-doun.   1028

995. MS. þrjnk.

Ho maẏ wiþ-holde him thouȝ he wolde
ffro wepẏng, ȝif þat he by-holde
And se Ihesu wepe so faste
And die for peẏne at þe laste.　　　　　　　1032
Loue, I praẏ þe now tak hede
Hose sides þou makest so sore to blede.

His name is above all praising.　His name is Ihesu, þe noble kẏng;
Þat name passeþ al oþer praẏsẏng.　　　　　1036
Whan I þat name Ihesu maẏ nemne
O poẏn[t] I haue of þe blisse of heuene.
Ihesu whan I haue in mẏ þouȝt
Al ertheIẏ blisse ẏ sette at nouȝt.　　　　　1040
Þou name ful of loue lẏkẏng,
I praẏ þe of non other thẏng
But þat þou wẏlt dwelle with me
And neuere out of mẏn herte fle.　　　　　1044
Seint Paul was tauȝt þorw þe holi gost
Þat Ihesu was of names most;
ffor whan heuene *and* erthe *and* helle also
Here þat name þeẏ knelon þer-to.　　　　　1048
Seint Peter seẏde þer-to þe same,
Þat soueraigne ouer alle is þat name;
fol. 45 b.　ffor onlẏ þorw þat name free
Mankẏnde in heuene hath geten a see.　　1052

It is the solace of saints.　Þis name is alle seintes solas,
A siker tour in euery cas.
It is a trompe of such a soun
Þat bereþ þe deueles mẏȝt a-doun.　　　　1056
Blessed be þat name of mẏȝt
Þat maẏ felle þe fend in fẏȝt.
Ihesu, þou makest oure foo to flee;
Swete name, blessed mot þou be.　　　　　1060

Jesus, write thy name in my heart.　Wrẏȝt, Ihesu, þi name of bote
Al with-inne mẏn herte-rote;
ffor I shal non enemẏ drede
As ofte as I þat name rede.　　　　　　　　1064
Whan I shal drawe toward mẏ deþ,
Whil me lasteþ speche and breþ

1038. MS. *poẏn.*

And I mowe þat name telle,
Þe fend with me maẏ not dwelle.   1068
Whan I here of þat name carpe,
Swetter it is þan anẏ harpe.
Þat name maẏ me murþe make,
Þat name maẏ mẏ serwe slake,   1072
þat name is ful of ioẏe and blis
þat name wot not what serwe is.
Ihesu is brennẏnge loue,
Ihesu is trompe of God aboue,   1076   That name is the trump of God.
Ihesu is oure hertes helthe,
Ihesu passeþ al wordlẏ welthe;
Ihesu is so swete a song   fol. 47 a.
Þer maẏ no mornẏng be among;   1080
Ihesu is swetter of sauour
Þan rose or lilie or anẏ oþer flour.
Ihesu is mercẏ and pite
To alle þo þat giltẏ be;   1084
Ihesu in sekenes is confort,
Ihesu in hele is oure disport;
Ihesu is so swete of soun,
It clenseþ þe eẏr of invẏroun.   1088
Þer maẏ now here no deuel dwelle
Þ[at] maẏ here of Ihesu telle.
Ihesu is al oure hertes hele,
Ihesu is al oure lẏues wele;   1092
Ihesu is more þan honẏ swete,
Ihesu maẏ oure bales bete;
Ihesu is angeles melodie,
Þei sesse not Ihesu to crẏe;   1096
Ihesu is shipmannes song,
Þe se-sterre þat wele not lede hem wrong.
As ofte as Ihesu nempned is,   It brings to man's aid all
Angeles ben redẏ þere, ẏwẏs;   1100   the nine orders of angels.
Seraphẏn, þat aungel cler,
Brennẏng brẏʒt he is redẏ þer;
Cherubẏn, þat aungel hẏe,
He comeþ ful redẏ to þat crẏe;   1104

1090. MS. þer.

	And aungels þat Trouns ẏ-cleped be,	
	ffor in hem is Godes owne se.	
fol. 47 b.	What man þeẏ here Ihesu calle,	
	Þere þeẏ ben ful redẏ alle.	1108
	Þer comeþ also from heuon adoun	
	Þe ordre of Domẏnacẏoun ;	
	Þe grete ost of Virtutes also,	
	Þei heron þat name and comon þer-to ;	1112
	Potestates, þat ordre of mẏʒt,	
	Comeþ a-doun with lem and lẏʒt ;	
	Of Principatus þe compenẏe	
	Comon a-doun wiþ melodẏe ;	1116
	Þanne comon Archangels redẏ dẏʒt,	
	And after hem Aungels brẏʒt.	
	Ihesu, þat name of mẏʒtes most,	
	Brẏngeþ with him his strong ost.	1120
	As ofte as Ihesu nempned be,	
	ffor drede þe fend begẏnneþ to fle ;	
	ffor alle þuse ordres of aungels brẏʒt	
	To bataẏle þeẏ ben redẏ dẏʒt ;	1124
	To Ihesu þeẏ knelon alle on kne	
	And askon him what his wille be,	
Now, love, thou knowest whom thou hast overcome.	Now, loue, þou knowest a partẏ On whom þou kẏndest þẏ maistrẏ.	1128
	ʒet and it þe forþinketh sore,	
	Þou art of loue to praẏse þe more.	
Repetition of the sufferings of Jesus.	I praẏ þe lok on him and se How mekelẏche he suffrede þe :	1132
	Alþeẏ þou do him serwe and wo,	
	He seẏth not ones, " Whẏ dost þou so ? "	
fol. 49 a.	Þe her of his hed is al to-drawe,	
	Þe bodẏ with scories al to-flawe ;	1136
	His hed with þornes al to-rent	
	To a knottẏ tre his bak is bent.	
	Wiþ rugged naẏles þe wrecches wode	
	Nailed him harde to þe rode.	1140
	Þus was þat lomb so meke and mẏlde	
	To-drawe and rent with wolues wilde.	
	Þanne wiþ-drow þe sunne his lẏʒt	
	And wolde not se þat delful sẏʒt ;	1144

Harde stones gonne to breste,
Dede bodies rẏson of hure reste;
And alle þẏnges on hure manere
ffor hure lord madon dredful chere,　　　1148
Saue wikked mannes herte a-lone　　　*Man alone*
Þat was harder þan anẏ stone;　　　*was unmoved.*
ffor þat ne hadde no pite
To sen his lord dion on tre.　　　1152
And þanne sẏ þe lord of blisse
Mannes grete vnkẏndenesse;
And þanne he wepte swẏthe sore,
More þan for wo þat was bẏ-fore.　　　1156
Ihesu, what hastou mẏsdo?
Whi shalt þou suffre serwe *and* wo?
Þou louedest wel in euerẏ nede,
Er loue haþ quẏt þe pus þẏ mede.　　　1160
God wolde þat I worthẏ were　　　*Would I were worthy*
ffor loue of þe to lion on bere;　　　*to die for Jesus.*
And whanne I þoȝte on þẏ deþ　　　*fol. 49 b*
ffor dele I sholde ȝiuon vp þe breþ.　　　1164
But I maẏ ben now ful sorẏ,
ffor I was neuere so worþẏ
On þat noble deþ to dẏe,
ffor þat deþ wole han a b[e]tter preie.　　　1168
Ho-so maẏ not han þo grace
With þat swete deþ to pase,
Al þe lẏf þat he hath here,
It nis but deþ withouten were.　　　1172
The maẏdon Marẏe, moder of grace,　　　*Mary's*
Sho lokede vp-on hure sones face　　　*sorrow at the crucifixion.*
And on his bodẏ blodẏ and bare;
Þanne was þat maẏdon ful of care.　　　1176
Sho lokede vp-on his forhed swote
And sẏ þe blod þer-on flete;
Þe mouth þat she hadde ofte ẏ-kust
Was ful of blod and spotel ẏ-drust;　　　1180
Sho saw þe face brẏȝt [of] ble
ffade and reulẏ onne to se;

1168. MS. bitter.　　　1181. MS. and.

32 Meditations on the Life and Passion of Christ

  ffor wo hure herte wex so cold
  It was worse þan deþ on hundredfold.   1184
  Moder, þin herte, what! it was wo
  To se þẏ sone blodẏ and blo
  Þat was sumtẏme so faẏr and swete
  Whanne he sok mẏlk of þẏ tete.   1188
  Strong was þẏ pẏne þe to wẏte
  His faẏre forhed with þornes wrẏte,
fol. 51 a.   His blisful brest with strokes shent,
  Hondes and fet with naẏles rent.   1192
  Ioẏful þou were whan he was born,
  But now is al þat ioẏe forlorn
  Wẏkked and fel is kẏnde of man,
  It doþ now þat it mẏȝte not þan.   1196
  Alas, þe beaute of his childhode,
  ffairer þan þe flour þat sprẏngeþ brode;
  Al þat it was to tendre þo,
  So mẏkel more is now his wo.   1200
  Þat time þou were of hẏm ful glad,
  And now þou art wiþ wo be-stad.
Death would   Now were deþ to þe ful dere,
have been
welcome to   ffor þẏ lif is not deþes pere;   1204
her.
  ffor peẏne of deþ is sone y-do,
  Peẏne of þe lẏf is not so.
  But now is deþ so ful of wreche
  Þat he wole not here þẏ speche;   1208
  Al-þeẏ þou him clepe and calle
  It nẏl not to þin herte falle;
  But he suffrede þe a lẏf to lede
  ffer werse þan anẏ deþes drede.   1212
  But þeẏ I wrẏte and speke euere,
  Hollẏ telle maẏ I neuere
  How ful þou were of serwe and wo
  To se þi sone ben serued so.   1216
Jesus gave   Ihesu, þou hẏnge on tre an hẏ
her into the
care of John.   And sẏ þẏ moder stonden þe nẏ.
  Þou lokedest reufullẏ hure vpon
  And toke hure to þẏ discẏple Ion;   1220
fol. 51 b.   And so þat swete maẏde Marẏe
  An oþer maẏdon haþ to gẏe.

Meditations on the Life and Passion of Christ

Þe maýdonhoþ of hem boþe to
Býnt hem in loue for euermo.   1224
Leue Ihesu, forsake not me,   *Jesus, that haddest*
Al-þeý I sýnful and gýltý be ;   *mercy on the thief, have*
ffor to [þe] þef þat heng þe bý   *mercy on me.*
Redeliche þou haddest mercý.   1228
Ihesu, þ[y] grete curtesýe
Makeþ me with trist on þe to crýe,
ffor wel I wot withouten drede
Þý mercy is more þan aný mýsdede.   1232
Ihesu, what herte maýst þou haue
Of þý fader mercý to craue
ffor þine enemýes stronge
Þat han spilt þý blod with wronge.   1236
To þi fader þý gost þou takest   *The death of Jesus.*
And þý lýf for wo forsakest.
Alas, whi ne mýȝte I dýe also,
Ihesu, whan I þenke on þý wo.   1240
Now is lif to deþ ý-falle,
Þe sonne sýkeþ and sterres alle,
Euel haþ medýcine ý-shent,
Þe se of loue is al ý-spent.   1244
Now maýst þou, sonne, and mone also,
Wepe *and* make serwe and wo,
ffor þat kýng þat made ȝou alle
Thorw dýnt of loue to grounde is falle ;   1248
Þe výne of ful gentel traille
Þorw gret tempest begýnneþ to faille ;
Þo grape þer-of þat was so god,   *fol. 53 a.*
It wascheþ in his owne blod.   1252
Now is for olde Adamis gýlt   *New Adam atones for*
Newe Adam with wrong ý-spýlt ;   *old Adam's guilt.*
Iosep is in a put bý-loke :
So ben his brederen on him ý-wroke.   1256
Þeý brengon his fader a reuful þýng,
Þe blodý cote of his derlýng.
Also, forsoþe, it nýs non other   *Abel is slain again.*
But Caým haþ slaýn Abel, his brother.   1260

1227. þe not in MS.   1229. MS. þc.

But þe ferste Abeles blod
Crýeþ wreche as it be wod;
Crýstes blod doþ al an oþer:
It crýeþ mercý for his brother. 1264
Alas, þis noble prýnce of prýs
Is take among his enemýs.
Iob is pouere and lýþ ful lowe,
Now wolon him not his frendes knowe; 1268
Now Machabeus, þat noble knýth,
Is feld a-doun in þat felle fýȝth;
Þe kýng Saul boþe felle and kene
Doþ kýng Dauid treý and tene. 1272

All joy and gladness depart. Now goþ aweý þe melodýe
Of harp and of sautrýe;
Þe·swete sýtole haþ lorn his soun;
Alle gamon and gle is leid adoun. 1276
Nou is lilie and rose in Maý
Boþe to-gýdere gon awaý.

fol. 53 b. Now-adaý in þe mornýnge
Briddes wille namore sýnge; 1280
Þe mone is gon a-waý fro nýȝt,
Þe sonne haþ lorn þe daýes lýȝt,
Þe cloudes hure leue han ý-take,
Lýf and solas han vs forsake. 1284
Alas, al mý while I spille
In þis caroýne to dwellon stille.
Nou lýf and loue is fro me gon,
How maý I leue here alon? 1288
Þou þat deiedest vpon þe tre,

Let me die with thee. Let me dýe also wiþ þe;
Let me neuer no lýkýng fýnde
Whil I shal dwellon þe be-hýnde, 1292
But leue in longýng and in trauaýle
Til I haue þe wiþ-outon faýle.

Slay in me earthly desires. Sle in me fleschlý lýkýng,
Veýn glorie and fals preýsýng. 1296
Sle desir of þe sýȝt,
ffor þat is aý to sýnne ý-dýȝt;
Hardnesse of herte and felonýe,
ffoule listes of lecherýe, 1300

Meditations on the Life and Passion of Christ

ffłesc[h]lẏ loue þat brenneþ so
And torneþ ate ende to serwe and wo.
Þat loue is cleped hate and grame, *A dispraising of fleshly love.*
Vnsauorẏ salt, preẏsẏng of blame, 1304
ffairnesse of fulthe, fruẏt of mornẏng,
ffaẏr sprẏng of daẏ and foul euenẏng,
Bẏtter honẏ and swete poẏson, fol. 55 a.
Stẏnkẏnd rose, feldand prẏson, 1308
Serful ioẏe and wepẏnge song,
[Bl]od-red lilie and rẏȝt of wrong,
Blak snow and loue of discord,
Pore richesse and bonde-lord, 1312
Sobrenesse boþ wilde and wod,
Bernẏnge baþ *and* harmful god,
A turtil clad in a wolues skẏn,
A culuer of þe lẏons kẏn, 1316
A nẏȝtẏngale wiþ an oxes þrote,
A þrostel w*ith* an asse note,
A flour wiþ galle al bẏ-gon,
Encense ẏ-mad al of brẏmston, 1320
Blẏnd fir gurd wiþ derknesse
Þ*a*t haþ brennẏng and no lẏȝtnesse.
Nou, herte, let þuse loues gon *Heart, love Christ alone.*
And set þẏ loue on Crẏst alon. 1324
Niȝt and daẏ where-so þou wende
Þi lord Ih*es*u þou haue in mẏnde.
It is ful lẏkẏng and ful lef
To suffre for his loue mẏschef, 1328
ffor ho-so is feld adoun for his loue,
Þanne is he most at his a-boue.
Mak me, Ih*es*u, glad to be
Simple and pore for loue of þe, 1332
And let me neue*re* for more nor lasse
Loue god to wel þat sone shal passe.
In mẏn herte aẏ mot it be, fol. 55 b. *May thy passion ever be imprinted in my heart.*
Þat ilke knottẏ rode-tre; 1336
Þe nailes and þe spere also
Þat þou were wiþ to deþe ẏ-do;

1301. MS. *fflescly.*   1310. MS. *Sod.*

The corone and þe scorges grete
Þat þou were wiþ so sore ẏ-bete; 1340
Þẏ wepẏng and þi woundes wẏde
Þe blod [þat] ran doun bẏ thi sẏde.
Þi shame, scorn, and gret despẏt,
Þe spotel þat fouled pẏ face whẏt, 1344
Þe eisel and þe bitter galle
And other of þẏ peẏnes alle;
But I haue hem in mẏ þouȝt
Al mẏ lẏf I sette at nouȝt. 1348

Love, write in my heart the sorrows of Mary,
Loue þat art so mẏkel of mẏȝt,
Writ in mẏn herte þat reuful sẏȝt,
To loke on þe maidon fre
Whan hure sone hẏng on þe rode-tre, 1352
And vpon þe knottẏ rode
Sho sẏ his sides breste on blode.
Al-þei mẏn herte be hard a[s] ston
Loue, ȝit þou mẏȝt wrẏte þer-on 1356
Wiþ nailes and wiþ spere kene,
So shullon þe lettres wel be sene.

and the sufferings of Jesus.
fol. 57 a.
Writ wel in mẏn herte depe
How Ihesu bẏgan to wepe 1360
Þo his bak was to þe rode bent,
With rogged nailes his hondes rent.
Writ þe strokes of hameres stoute,
Writ þe blod rennẏng a-boute. 1364
Þe nailes stẏnton at þe bon;
Þo was Ihesu ful wo-bẏgon.

Write the crowning;
Writ þe kẏnges coronement,
How þornes on his hed weron bent 1368
A fals se[r]uant his lord now sleþ,
And kẏng of lẏf dampne[þ] to deþ.
Writ also his speches swete
Whan þo traẏtour him gan to grete. 1372
Þat tretor was ful of þe fend
And ȝet he clepede him his frend.

the trial before Pilate;
Writ hou he was boundon sore
And drawe forþ Pilate to-fore; 1376

1342. þat not in MS.   1355. MS. *aston.*
1369. MS. *seuant.*   1370. MS. *dampned.*

How sweteliche an[s]werede he þo
To him þat was his felle fo.
Writ þat kyng þat quencheth care,
Hou he stant naked wiþ sydes bare. 1380
He þat 3eueþ robes ful wyde
Now haþ no cloþ to kouere his side.
Loue, I pray þe eft-sones writ
Þat noble kyng with body so whit 1384
Þat clo[þ]e[d] al þe firmament,
Naked stant at iugement.
Writ him naked þat leneth loue   fol. 57 b.
To aungels alle þat ben a-boue; 1388
ffor in þat ilke swete sy3t
Is al hure ioye, hure grace, hure my3t.
Writ after þis þat body swete,   the torment-
Wiþ sharpe scories þat body bete. 1392   ing;
Þat fayre face wax red for shame;
Scornyng þey made of hym hure game.
Writ also þat fayre face
Byspat ful foule in þat place. 1396
ffor gret shame of þat vylonye
Doun to gronde he cast his ye.
Writ peynes, scornes, and despyt,
The rede woundes on skyn so whyt, 1400
Ley3henge and hidynge of his sy3t,
And al a-bobbynge of þe kyng of my3t.
Writ hou Herodes cloþed him al in whit,
ffor þat was signe of gret despit. 1404
He sente him a3eyn to Pilate,
And he made Ihesu ful mate.
Þanne dede he of his cloþes alle
And clad him in a purpul palle. 1408
Þei kneledon a-doun þe lord by-forn
And cleþedon him kyng al on hure scorn.
Writ þat ilke fals enqueste   the cry for
Þat cryedon ay without reste; 1412   crucifixion;
" Hang him on þe rode-tre,
ffor he wole kyng of Iewes be."

1377. MS. *an werede* with a mark for the insertion of a letter
between the separated syllables.   1385. MS. *clodeþ*; cf. v. 940.

38 Meditations on the Life and Passion of Christ

fol. 59 a.
the shame
of Jesus;

Writ vpon mẏn herte-bok
Þat swete kẏnges reulẏ lok 1416
ffor shame of þat hidous crẏ,
Þat woldon of him haue no mercẏ.
Writ hou he stod as lomb so stille
And suffred hem don with him hure wille. 1420
Þe lomb liȝth stille under þe knẏf
And spekeþ not for his owne lẏf.
Writ hou whan þe croẏs was broȝt
And þe nailes of ẏron wroȝt 1424
Ihesu began to chẏuere and quake;
His herte was wo þeẏ he not spake.
Writ how he gan dou[n]ward loke
Whan þe Iewes hẏm his croẏs toke. 1428
He bar it forþ wiþ reulẏ chere,
The teres ronnon adoun bẏ his lere.

the fierce-
ness of the
Jews;

Writ þe Iewes, þe hondes felle,
How þeẏ gonnon to crẏe and ȝelle 1432
Vp-on Ihesu, þe kẏng so fre,
Whan Pilat him dampned ded to be.
Writ hou hungrẏ wolues wode
Þe lomb to-rend and soukon his blode; 1436
And ȝet ne ben þeẏ not so felle
As ben þe Iewes, soþ to telle;
ffor Baraban, þe stronge þef,
Was to hem lẏkẏng and lef, 1440
And him þat dede neuere ille
Þeẏ weron wod his blod to spille.

fol. 59 b.

Writ turmentoures ful redẏ sent
ffor to a-bẏdon þe iuggement; 1444
Croẏs and nail, coron and þorn,
fful redẏ þeẏ haddon dẏȝt a-forn.
Whan dom was ȝiue aȝeẏn þat kẏng,
Þere was lauȝtre, crẏ, and scornẏng. 1448
Þe sharpe þornes weron sone ẏ-fet
And hẏe vpon his hed ẏ-set.
Writ how þe Iewes weron glad
Whan þeẏ sion his blod shad. 1452
Writ how muche was his mẏschief
Whan þeẏ ascrẏedon hẏm as a þef.

1427. MS. *douward*.

Writ his swete moders wo   *Mary's woe*
Whan sho sẏ hẏm to dede go.   1456
I-wẏs þeẏ þou write al þẏ lẏue
Þou sholdest neuere hure wo dẏscrẏue.
Ioẏe of hure herte was al ẏ-lorn
Whan sho saẏ þe sharpe þorn   1460
Makẏng blodẏ þat louelẏ lere
Þat was to hure lef and dere.
Whan sho sẏ þat child ẏ-strept
Þat sho hadde so ȝong ẏ-kept,   1464
ffor reuthe and wo sho ful a-doun
And laẏ stille a[s] deþ in swoun.
Writ his bodẏ with blod ẏ-spreẏnt   *the wounded body of*
As is þe welkene with sterres ẏ-peẏnt;   1468 *Jesus.*
Or as is þe medwe in Maẏ   *fol. 61 a.*
Bẏset wiþ manẏ a flour ful gaẏ.
Writ þe kẏng þat is so wẏs
Of a tretour sold for lẏtẏl prẏs.   1472
Coueitẏse, aẏ worþ þe wo,
Þi-self þou slest, þeẏ non oþer do.
Writ hou his fon kemon on a ras
And maden til hẏm ful fel manas,   1476
And shewdon him boþe naẏl and tre
On whẏch he sholde hanged be.
But stille he stod and wolde not speke;
Þe teres ronnon bẏ his cheke;   1480
ffor alle assentedon him to sle,
No man of him wolde haue pẏte.
Loue, ȝet writ wel in mẏn herte,
How blod out of his woundes sterte.   1484
Loue, writ with þi blod so ofte   *Write, love, until my*
Min harde herte tẏl it be softe.   *heart is soft.*
Writ now, loue, þou prẏnce of prẏs
Þat is so worþẏ and so wẏs,   1488
Swete of speche, curteẏs and hende,
He takeþ his leue a-weẏ to wende.
Corteẏs kẏng, so wel were we
Miȝte we ben ded and gon with þe.   1492

1466. MS. *al.*

But now I dwelle and þou art gon;
I-wis, I ne wot what I shal don.
Writ his herte drury and drad,
To-fore Pylat þo he was lad. 1496

Writ his boundless love.
Writ his loue þat was so strong,
Þat made him to suffre so mukel wrong,
And for vnkynde mannes sake
Made him dredful deþ to take. 1500
His body was beton and gan to blede,
His herte colded and quok for drede.
Writ now, loue, þat I may knowe
What loue to Ihesu þat I owe. 1504
Al-þey I fro him fle
He folweþ ay to sauon me.

Write his death.
Writ his deþ so ful of myȝt,
It ȝeueþ strengthe to man in fyȝt. 1508
Ho-so may haue þat deþ in þouȝt
Þe fend ne may nyȝhe him noȝt.
Writ hou þey hidon his face
And a-bobbedon þe kyng of grace; 1512
His her þey renton al awey:
Acursed was þat ilke play.
Þey seton adoun vpon a plot
And on his cloþes drowen lot, 1516
And he hung nakud vp-on þe tre:
A reuful syȝthe was þat to se.

Nail, who gave thee leave to draw his blood?
Þou nail of yron, who ȝaf þe leue
Blod of þe flour for to reue? 1520
Whi þorlest þou þat fayre roser
And þe lilie so whyt and cler?
Now þou hast ioye at þi wille,
ffor of þat blod þou drynkest þy fille. 1524
Hadde I þer-of a drope y-wis,
Kepte I neuere of more blis.

fol. 63 a.
Loue, I pray þe eftsones writ
Þe rede blod on skyn so whit, 1528
Gronynge, sykynge, serwe, and care,
And shame to stonde naked bare.

Such writing makes a book of
Loue, with such noble wrytyng
Þou makest a bok of gret lykyng. 1532

Meditations on the Life and Passion of Christ

What týme I rede þat bok a-rýȝt
Þanne am I glad, ioyful, and lýȝt ;
Whan I speke of þat kýng so fre
I mot nedes ioýful be ; 1536
But whan I þenke hou he is ded,
Mý wele is went, I can no red.
But I mot ȝet a lýtýl stounde
Morne for þat depe wounde. 1540
Writ now, loue, how water sterte
fforþ with þe blod out of his herte.
Þat is water of gret lýkýng,
It makeþ frouýt of loue to sprýng ; 1544
And þe soþe for to telle,
Þat water quencheþ þe fier of helle,
And sýnne þat makeþ þo soule vnclene,
Þorw mýȝt þerof is not sene. 1548
Writ, loue, hou þat lord so fre
Bereþ on his bak þe rode-tre
And goþ to-ward his turnement
Berýng his owne iuggement. 1552
With strokes of scories and poýnt of þorn
Muche of his blod he haþ for-lorn.
He wex feýnt and gan to felde
And wente not faste al as þeý wolde. 1556
Þanne weron his fon redý and prest
And shouon him forþ without rest ;
With punches and strokes þeý dedon him go ;
Sore weþ þat lord for wo. 1560
Writ hou he was led on hý
Vpon þe mount of Caluerý ;
And þere was þe lord so fre
Hanged vpon þe rode-tre ; 1564
And so ful dere þat lord aboȝte
Þe wikkede werkes þat Adam wroȝte.
ffor an appel þat Adam et
Ihesu oure lord his lýf for-let. 1568
Adam sý þat appel-tre,
Noble of fruýt and faýr to se,
And for þat tre so swete of sýȝt
On rode-tre Ihesu is pýȝt. 1572

great delight.

Write now the water flowing from Jesus' side.

Write the march to Calvary ;

fol. 63 b.

and the crucifixion.

Writ, loue, his strong trauaẏle
þat he hadde in þo bataẏle.
fful harde and sore he hadde swonken;
He wax a-þurst and wolde han dronken. 1576
Þei putten a sponge vp-on a spere,
Eẏsel and galle þer-inne were.
To his mouþ þat spere þeẏ þruste
And beden him drẏnke, ȝẏf him leste. 1580
Of þat drẏnk he tok asaẏ
And turned also swẏde þe hed awaẏ.
fful sore he gan to grone also
And seẏde, "Now is al ẏ-do." 1584

Write Jesus' battle on the cross.
fol. 65 a.

Writ now, loue, þat kẏng of mẏȝt
In red armure is shape to fẏȝt;
Withouton stedes and hors of prẏs
He haþ ouercomon his enemẏs. 1588
Ihesu, þou hast no trompes loude
Sheld of gold ne crestes proude,
Ne brunẏe brẏȝt ne haberioun,
Ne brẏȝt swerd ne fel fauchoun. 1592
The hors þat þou onne rẏdest
Þou þorlest not with spores his sẏdes.
Brẏȝt armure hast þou non;
In þis bataile þou fẏȝtest alon. 1596
Þou ridest vp-[on] a selẏ asse
Aȝeẏne þe deueles grẏslẏ tasse.
So sleþ þo coluer þe serpent,
Þe lomb haþ þe wolf ẏ-hent. 1600
In stude of an helm so brẏȝt
Corone of þornes to þe is dẏȝt;
Þin haberion is þẏ bodẏ fre,
Þẏ baner is þe rode-tre. 1604

Write these pains in my heart, that earthly suffering may seem light.

Writ, loue, in mẏn herte so
Þuse peẏnes and other mo,
Þat whan I haue hem in my þouȝt,
What-so I suffre it greueþ me noȝt. 1608
Ȝif I be low for his loue
Þan am I most at mẏn aboue.

1597. *On* not in MS.

ffastẏng [i]s feste, mornẏng [i]s blis,
ffor his loue pouerte is rẏches ; 1612
Þo harde haire is more of pris
Þan purpul or pal, pelure or grẏs ;
Defaute for his loue is plente, fol. 65 b.
And likẏng lẏf ded to be. 1616
ȝif I be with wo bẏ-stad
ffor his loue, þanne am I glad ;
To suffre scornes and dispẏt
ffor loue of him is gret delẏt. 1620
Swete kẏng of mẏȝtes most,
In mẏn herte put þi gost,
Þat I mot fulfulle in dede
Þuse þinges þat I speke and rede. 1624
Lat me fele what ioẏe it be
To suffre wo for loue of þe ;
How swete it is for the to wepe,
How softe in haẏre forte slepe. 1628
Let now loue his bowe bende,
An arwe to mẏn herte sende,
Þat it maẏ perce to þe rote ;
ffor such a wounde were mẏ bote. 1632
Make me, Ihesu anẏȝt to wake
And in mẏ mouþ þat name take ;
And wheþer þe nẏȝt were short or long,
Let Ihesu euere be mẏ song. 1636
Let swete preẏer a cheẏne be   Let prayer
To drawe Crist adoun of his se,   be a chain to
                                        draw Christ
Þat I maẏ make him a dwellẏng   to my heart.
In mẏn herte at his lẏkẏng. 1640
Þer he shal ben with loue ẏ-fed,
A clene saule shal ben his bed.
Rest in swetnesse he shal so take
Þat wordles malice him not awake. 1644
Þere shal ben cluppẏng and kussẏng   fol. 67 a.
ffor gret loue of þat comelẏ kẏng.
Out fro þat hous shal he not wende
But dwellon þere wiþ-outen ende ; 1648 There he
                                        shall dwell
                                        without end.

1611. MS. *as* twice.

44 Meditations on the Life and Passion of Christ

    And þere ne shal no wordles gyle,
    No wrenches, ne no fendes wyle
    Make þat swetnesse awaẏ to gon,
    But it shal laste euere in on.   1652
    Þe sparres of þat chambre fre
    Of sipresse þanne shulle þeẏ be.
    Þe postes shulle be of ẏuer,
    Þe rof peẏnted with sterres cler.   1656

The soul, Jesus' wife, shall delight in his presence.
    Þere shal þe saule, Ihesus wẏf,
    In gret lẏkẏng ledon hure lẏf
    Hure blisse shal ben al in þe sẏȝt
    Of hure hosebondes face brẏȝt.   1660
    Whan sho seþ his faẏre face
    And feleþ swetnesse of his grace,
    And his godnesse haþ in hure þouȝt,
    Al er[þ]ly blisse sho set at nouȝt.   1664
    Sho sẏngeþ to him a loue-song
    And wepeþ also euer among.
    Sẏngẏng he mot teres lete
    ffor ioẏe of him þat is so swete.   1668
    He shal ben lẏk þe lẏtel bee
    Þat sekeþ þe blosme on þe tre
    And soukeþ on þe prumorole
    Þat is wiþouton wem or mole.   1672

fol. 67 b.
    He shal entre in-to þat seler
    Þat is ful of wẏn so cler,
    Þat þeẏ he drẏnke þer-of euere
    So muche it is hure wel þe leuere.   1676
    Tel now, swete kẏng of lẏf,
    Som of þi counsail to þi wẏf ;
    Hit shal hure loue mukel eche
    Ȝif þou wolt hure of loue teche.   1680

Let the soul love none but Jesus.
    Let hure loue noþing in londe
    But only Ihesu hure hosebonde.
    Al other blisse and other beaute,
    Be it serwe to hure and foul to se ;   1684
    ffor al oþer ioẏe and blis
    Serwe and wo forsoþe it is,

1664. MS. *erly*.   1667. See Intro., p. xvi, Note 3.

And lasteþ but a lytel while,
Mannes soule to be-gyle.   1688
But whar-to speke I of þis blis?
It doubleþ al mẏ wo, ẏ-wẏs;
ffor whiles I bere þis bodẏ a-boute
Al ioẏe and blisse I am wiþoute.   1692
I bere a bodẏ maud of molde
Þat clopeth me with cares colde;
[Þer]fore I mot lete blisse go
And turne aȝeẏn to wor[d]le of wo,   1696
And telle wiþ carful romaunce   But I must
More of Ihesu harde penaunce,   speak again
                                            of Jesus'
And speke of spere, nailes, and þorn   suffering.
Þat his bodẏ was wiþ torn.   1700
And, loue, I bidde þe a bone,   fol. 69 a.
                                            Love, write
Þat þou write in mẏn herte sone   first the
Þe peẏne of Iob and al his speche,   sorrows of
                                            Job.
Whan his fon tokon of him wreche.   1704
ffor Iob þat suffred gret afraẏ
Bẏtokeneþ Crist as he wel maẏ.
His pouerte and his penaunce
He suffred with hertlẏ suffraunce.   1708
Iob þat was wittẏ and wẏs
Seẏde to his enemẏs;
'Of mẏ bodẏ ȝe make a mark   Job's com-
                                            plaint
And shote to me strokes stark.   1712 against his
Blodẏ and bare I stonde stille   enemies.
And suffre ȝow don with me ȝoure wille.
Stille I stonde and harde I wepe
And alle ȝoure harde strokes kepe.   1716
With harde bondes ȝe han me bounde
And on mẏ bodẏ maud manẏ a wounde,
And in mẏ face þat was so whit
Ȝe spatton alle with gret dispẏt.   1720
Curour was þere neuer non
Þat mẏȝte a-weẏ so faste gon
As don þe daẏes of mẏ lẏf
Þat passen a-weẏ with wo and strẏf.   1724

        1695. MS. *Bẏfore*.   1696. MS. *worle*.

Mine breþeren alle han me forsake
And mȳne fomen han me take.
On me þeẏ taken a fals quest
And beton me wiþouton rest, 1728
Am I not mad of flesch and bon
And neẏþer of bras ne of ston?
I nam no wal of þe salte se;
Alas, whi fare ȝe þus with me? 1732
God wot I dede ȝou neuer ille
And ȝet I haue of wo mẏ fille."

Write the prophets' sayings about Jesus.

Writ now, loue, prophetes sawes
Þat weron said bẏ olde dawes. 1736
Tak hed to hure wordes alle,
ffor now in dede þeẏ ben falle.
Þei toldon of his Natẏuẏte
And of [his] deþ on rode-tre, 1740
Of his serwe and of his wo;
Þou mẏȝt wel se now it is so.
Writ þat nẏȝt þat he was take
And wiþ turmentoures bẏwake 1744

Write of Jesus' face disfigured by torment.

Dim wexon his ẏon cler;
Shame chanẏeth al his cher.
He was so be-seẏn with peẏne a þrowe
Þat his frendes coude him not cnowe. 1748
Þei asked war þis be Ihesu swete
Þat is þus with scories bete.
Wher is his face as lilie cler,
His lippes lẏk a red roser? 1752
Alas, whi makeþ þat louelẏ lere
So delful and so reuful chere?

Contrasts of Jesus' power "yesterday" and "to-day."

Wher Ihesu shul neuer more
Don as he dede afore? 1756
Ȝesterdaẏ swete was his speche
Wan he wolde vs his lore teche;
To-daẏ he is to baẏ y-broȝt,
Standẏng stille he spekeþ noȝt. 1760
He haþ no cloþ to keuere him wiþ,
He stand stan-naked lẏm and liþ.

1740. *his* not in MS.

Ȝesterdaẏ he coude angels teche;
To-daẏ he spareþ al his speche.   1764
Ȝesterdaẏ he ȝaf corone of gloryẏe
To hem þat haddon þe victoryẏe;
To-daẏ his her is of yẏ-torn
And he is coroned with a thorn.   1768
I herde him-self a vyẏne calle;
To-day he dryẏnketh eẏsel and galle.
Ȝesterdaẏ he sente þe sonne his lyẏȝt;
To-daẏ þeẏ han hud al his syẏȝt.   1772
Ȝesterdaẏ he was myẏrie and glad;
To-daẏ he is wiþ wo byẏ-stad.
Þanne comeþ þer forþ a good womman   (The Ver-
And reuþe haþ of þat ryȝtful man.   1776   nacle.)
Wiþ a cloþ his face sho wipte,
Þe forme þer-of þe cloþ him clipte.
Ȝesterdaẏ he made alle halwen glad;
To-daẏ he is on þe rode sprad.   1780
fful sore he seẏde, "I am a-þurst;"
And galle is to his mouþ þrist.
Ȝesterdaẏ he gẏed sonne and se;
To-daẏ he hangeþ on rode-tre.   1784
Al þẏng he made with his grace;
Now haþ his hed no restyẏng-place.
Ȝut maẏ not deþ his loue slake.   fol. 71 b.
Alas, why hath loue hyẏm forsake?   1788
fforsake he is of frend and foo   He is for-
And don to deþe with serwe and wo.   saken of
He þat is of treuthe welle   friend and
Hangeþ bẏtwene defes felle.   1792   foe.
Þis is aȝeyẏns alle lawes—
ffalsnesse and trewthe to ben felawes.
Wo auȝte hem be and sore drede
Þat han maud þat felawrede.   1796
Bẏhold þat lord of myẏȝtes most,
Wiþ wepyẏng he ȝelt vp þe gost.
Þe soule is fro þe bodẏ gon
And lowe he is yẏ-leẏd vnder a ston. 1800
As turtel morneþ for his make
So don ful manẏ for cristes sake.

<small>Write Jesus' words, "If they do this in the green tree—" (See Luke xxiii 31)</small>

Writ, loue, a swete word also
þat Ihesu seýde in al his wo; 1804
"Siþþe þei don þus in grene tre
Whan it sereþ how shal it be?"
Þis word is als mukel to seýn
As, "Siþþe þei putten me to peýn 1808
Now wil mý gode werkes ben grene,
Here-after þei wollon don werse, ý wene."
Writ also, loue, þe rode-tre
þat wroȝt was in dýspýt to be; 1812
Nou it is woxe of bounte best
And kýng it makeþ on hed *and* brest.

<small>fol. 73 a. Jesus' love was undaunted by death.</small>

I not wheþer I maý wel leue
þat aný deþ him myȝte greue; 1816
ffor he was so wiþ loue ý-bounde,
He ȝaf no fors [of dedes wounde].
Loue him comaundeþ at his wille
And Ihesu is redý to forþfulle; 1820
And loue is fers and wol not spare
Til he haue mad his bodý bare.
Loue makeþ his siþes renne on blode
And hangeþ him vp-on þe rode. 1824
Loue bond so him he mýȝte not fle
Til he were nailed vp-on þe tre.

<small>Why would Jesus thus embrace death?</small>

Whý wolde he abrod his armes sprede
And býclippe[n] þe deþ so ful of drede? 1828
Alas, whý was þat lord so swete
So glad wit*h* dredful deþ to mete?
Whi is lýȝt cast in-to derknesse?
Whi haþ þe flour lorn his fairnesse? 1832
Whi shal þe výne drýnkon galle?
Whi wepeþ þo [y]e brýȝtest of alle?
Whi is [i]t so graue, þe hous of ýuer?
Whi is it so hors, þe voýs so cler? 1836
Whi dieþ þe whete vnder þe chaf?
Where is þat aungels mete ȝaf?
Þe mete of lýf, whi is it lene?
Þe brýȝte face, whi is it not sene? 1840

<small>1803. MS. *a swete a word.* 1818. MS. *dedes of wounde.*
1828. MS. *býclipped.* 1834. MS. *þe.* 1835. MS. *st.*</small>

Meditations on the Life and Passion of Christ 49

Whi is he wiþ nailes shut
That brak þe ȝates of helle-put?
Whi hangeþ he vpon an helle   fol. 78 b.
Þat hangeþ helles at his wille?   1844
Whi hangeþ he on tre so pale   Why does he who made trees, hang upon the tree?
Þat made trees boþe grete and smale?
Whi shal now þe swete lomb,
Swetter þan þe honý-comb,   1848
Withouten skele forgo his lýf
And quake for drede vnder þe knýf?
Whi wole þat stronge vnýcorn
Þat was of þat maýdon born   1852
Make his bed vpon a tre
And stike þerc-onne wiþ naýles þre?
Whi is þat noble senatour
Of cheualrý þat bereþ þe flour   1856
Þus wrongfullý feld to grounde
And bý-bled wiþ depes wounde?
Whi welkeþ now þe rose of prýs?
Whi fadeþ þo lilie of paradýs?   1860   Why fades the lily of paradise?
Whi doþ wermot þe lilie harm?
Whi dieþ þe spouse in þe wýfes arm?
Whi wereþ he now þe corone of þorn
Þat was coroned wiþ gold to-forn?   1864
Whi is þe welle of al swetnesse
Medle[d] with bale and bitternesse?
Whi haþ galle with honý to done?
Whi sleþ venýin þe kýnges sone?   1868
What skile haþ þe lord of liȝt
To haue a cloude to keuere his siȝt?
Whi sholde þe child of Marie [b]ore   fol. 75 a.
Wiþouten gilt ben so for-lore?   1872
Alas, what eýlen þe woundes of wreche
So to slen hure owne leche?
How mýȝte aný dedes wounde
ffelle so noble a kýng to grounde?   1876
His woundes bledon on euerý halue,
To hem leide no man salue;

    1866. MS. *medleþ*.
    1871. MS. *b* almost entirely rubbed out.
PASSION OF CHRIST   E

No man wesch þe blod hem fro
No man wolde rewe on his wo. 1880

It was love made Jesus suffer.
Thus was Ihesu wiþ loue take
And suffred wo for oure sake,
And ȝaf vs ensample also
ffor loue of him to suffre wo. 1884
Loue, þou hast bounden þe kẏng
Þat is lord ouer alle þẏng,
And send him to vs hider adoun
To dwelle wiþ vs in oure prisoun. 1888
It semeþ þou art more of mẏȝt
Þan is Ihesu þe kẏng of rẏȝt.
To dispute þat wole I not dwelle,
Anẏ sortaẏn þer-of to telle. 1892

God and love are one.
But þis wot I wel forsoþe,
On substaunce þeẏ ben boþe;
Euon honour and euon blis
Boþe þei han, wiþouten mẏs. 1896
ffor þe bok seẏth þat God is loue
Þat cam adoun fram heuene aboue.

fol. 76 b.
I saẏ, alas, he goþ a-waẏ
Þat swetter is þan rose in Maẏ. 1900
Writ in me, loue, his swete brest
In wich þou haddest al þi rest.
It was ful of counseẏl good,
It dieþ now in his owne blod; 1904
And þei I be fer þer-fro
And bodelẏ maẏ not comon þer-to,
Wiþ gret desir of herte, ẏ-wis,
I shal it boþe cluppe and kus; 1908
And whan I haue it in mẏ þoȝt,
Þei deþ come, I drede him noȝt.

Write the pitiful appearance of Jesus.
Writ þe kẏnges lippes to
Whan he toward his deþ gan go; 1912
ffor drede hou þei gonne to quake,
As doþ þe lef whan wẏndes wake
Se hou he hangeþ on þe rode;
Se hou his sides gon on blode; 1916
Se hou his hed hangeþ ful lowe;
Se hou no man wol him knowe.

Meditations on the Life and Passion of Christ 51

Writ, loue, þat I maẏ singe þis laẏ,		A song of mourning for Jesus' departing.
Mornẏng for his wendẏng awaẏ.	1920	
Lo, now he goþ aweẏ fro me,		
Swetter þan is þe blosme on tre,		
Þe violet and þe rose-flour		
Boþe þei luson hure colour;	1924	
Þe harp haþ lorn his swete soun;		
The nẏȝtẏngale liþ in prisoun.		
Lo, now he goþ, þe mẏȝtful kẏng,		fol. 77 a.
In siȝt of whom is more lẏkẏng	1928	
Þan vp to heuene for to stẏe.		
But ho-so mẏȝte sen him wiþ ẏe,		
Ȝif þo þat ben in helle-put		
In strong prisoun harde beshut,	1932	
Miȝte þei se his ioẏful chere,		
Al hure penaunce delẏuered were,		
Lo, now he goþ, þe duk so fre,		
fful of grace and of beaute.	1936	
His presence plesseþ man so,		Saints, martyrs, and learned clerks bear witness to the joy of his presence: Steven,
It ouercomeþ alle serwe and wo.		
Þat witnesset wel seẏnt Steuene		
Whan he sẏ Ihesu on hẏ in heuene;	1940	
Þo greuede him not þe stones fele,		
Þat suþþe was so ful of wele.		
Peter proued þis also		Peter,
Whan he was on þe rode do.	1944	
Glad he was to dẏe on tre		
Ones to se þat face fre.		
Also þe holẏ pope Clement,		Clement,
He dredde neuer no turment	1948	
Whan he was in þe se a-queẏnt;		
Alle his cares weron a-queẏnt.		
Also Iohan euangelẏst		John the Evangelist,
Was soden in oẏle for loue of Crist	1952	
Paule apostel bereþ witnes		Paul,
Þat Ihesu is so ful of blis;		
And þe noble marter Laurence		fol. 77 b. Lawrence,
Such lẏkẏng haþ in his presence	1956	

1949. For *a-queẏnt* of MS. read *a-dreẏnt*.

	He felte not þe hete of þe fýr,	
	So brennend was his desýr.	
Vincent,	Also Výncent, þe stronge knýth,	
	He was neuere felt in fýȝt;	1960
	As glad he was wounded to be	
	As shipman is of sterre in se.	
	Þat sheweth Ierom, þat noble klerk,	
	And preueþ it in al his werk;	1964
	And oþer clerkes also couþe,	
	Seýnt Ion with þe gildon mouþe,	
	Bernard, Gregor, Ambros, Dionýs,	
	Alle þeý weron clerkes of pris	1968
	And of holinesse þei beren gret name,	
	And alle þei witnessen þe same.	
St. Thomas of Canterbury,	Þe archebischop, seýnt Thomas,	
	Þer-fore suffred a rulý ras;	1972
	Vp-on his hed rede men maý	
	Þat he ne dradde aný afraý.	
St. Katherine,	Katerýne, þe maidon clene,	
	Dredde noȝt þe wheles kene.	1976
St. Margaret,	Þe holý maidon, Margarete,	
	Þoȝte for loue hure peýnes swete.	
Mary Magdalene,	Magdelaýn so ful of loue,	
	Þat hadde hure fode from heuen aboue—	1980
	In þe roche hure lif sho ladde—	
	ffor no penaunce sho ne dradde.	
fol. 79 a.	Loue of Ihesu it is so strong,	
	It dredeþ neider wo ne wrong.	1984
St. Dominic,	Seint Domenik gan þat to teche,	
	And bad his breþeren so to teche;	
	He haþ of Crist ensample take	
	Wordes blisse to forsake.	1988
St. Francis,	Seint Fraunceis doþ þer-wiþ acorde,	
	Þat goþ knet with a knottý corde;	
	Þe knotte býtokneþ stedefast loue	
	Þat knetteþ him to God aboue;	1992
St. Augustine.	Seint Austýn þat was so wýs,	
	Among doctours he bereþ þe pris;	
	His trewe lore is of gret mýȝt,	
	Shýnýng as þe sterre brýȝt;	1996

He bereþ wel witnesse of þis þing,
Þat in Ihesu is al lykyng.
Siþþen many þou fyndest seyntes in heuone
Beron witnesse of al my steuene.   2000
Þer Ihesu is, þei tellon alle,
Þer may neuer wo by-falle.
Lo, now he goþ þat haþ pyte
On hem þat dedon him on þe tre.   2004
Of his fader he prayde grace
ffor hem þat spatton in his face.
Lo, now, loue, hou þin hosebounde
With deþ is exiled out of londe.   2008
Where shalt þou an oþer fynde   *Where will love find such another?*
Swich on as he was and so kynde?
His syde is wiþ a spere y-cleft;   *fol. 79 b.*
Ther is no blod in him by-left;   2012
In his body now is no space
Where þou myʒt han þi restyng-place.
His body is al wiþ blod by-gon,
Byset with woundes many on;   2016
Þe woundes ben so felle and fele
Þer is no man þat may hem hele.
Ihesu þat gost with loue y-bounde   *Jesus, be with me at*
And suffrest for me many a wounde,   2020 *my dying.*
At my dying visite me
And mak þe fend a-way to fle.
ffor þi semblant þat is so bryʒt,
Derknes þer-aʒeyns haþ no myʒt,   2024
But al fulþe fleþ away
As doþ þe nyʒt at þe lyʒt of þe day,
Lord þat art so lef and dere,
Dispise not my pore preiere;   2028
ffor Paul þat was so fel and wod
To spille Cristen menues blod,
To þe wolde he no preier make
And ʒet þou woldest him not forsake.   2032
Þou myʒt not þanne forsake me
Siþþe þat I praye to þe.

2009. MS. *and.*

54 Meditations on the Life and Passion of Christ

   At my dẏing I hope, ẏ-wẏs,
   Of þi presence shal I not mẏs ;   2036
   Þan shalt þou make me to rẏse
   ffrom deþ to lẏue on such a wẏse
fol. 81 a As þou arise on Esterdaẏ
   In ioẏe and blisse to lẏuon aẏ.   2040

The Resur- Þat swete resurectẏoun
rection.
   Haþ broken helles strong prisoun,
   And with manẏ a blodẏ wounde
   Þe prisoners þou hast vn-bounde.   2044

Appearance Whan þou were arise to lẏue
to Mary
Magdalene, To Marie Magdeleẏn ful blyve
a token of
Jesus'mercy. Bi-fore alle other þou woldest apere
   In token sho was þo luf and dere.   2048
   And sho þat was sẏnful bi-fore,
   Whan sho let of and dede namore,
   More sẏne of loue þou shewedest þi-selue
   To hure þan to þe aposteles twelue.   2052
   Ihesu, mukel is þi godnesse,
   Þou makest such a sẏkernesse
   Þat þi mercẏ ful redẏ is
   To alle þo þat don amẏs :   2056
   What tẏme man askeþ þi mercẏ
   Wiþouten faile it is redẏ.

Appearance Whan þou were out of dedes boundes
to the
disciples. Þou shewedest alle þi wẏde woundes,   2060
   And þi side þat was so opon
   Þou bad seint Thomas to gropon,
   And bad him whil þat his lif last
   He shulde ben trewe and stedefast   2064
   ffor to bẏleuon withouton strẏf
   Þat þou were rise from deþ to lẏf.
fol. 81 b. Þo com þou to þi disciples alle
   And ete with hem in an halle,   2068
   And speke to hem with mẏlde steuene,
The Ascen- And stẏ so vp in-to heuene.
sion.
   Þe holẏ gost þou sendest adoun
   Amonges hem with sodeẏn soun,   2072
   Þat tauȝte he[m] alle manere speche
   And make hem bold þe feẏȝt to teche.
       2073. MS. hel.

Þanne toke þou vp þi moder swete
And madest hure in heuene a sete ; 2076 The Assumption of Mary.
Quen of quenes, ladẏ of mẏȝt,
Souereẏn ouer al, as it is rẏȝt,
And as [I] bẏ-leue wel
Bodẏ and soule, flesch and fel, 2080
Sho was vp to heuon take,
As I can þer-to skiles make.
ffor sho was out of sẏnnes clene,
Þere was no wem in hure sene. 2084
It semeþ al aȝeẏns resoun The incorruptibility of Mary's body.
Sho shulde turne to corrupcẏoun ;
And siþþe þat Crist, þe lord of lẏȝt,
Tok of hure his bodẏ so brẏȝt, 2088
Hure bodẏ was of þe same kẏnde—
To wermes mete hou mẏȝte it wende ?
Þe hie kẏng of rẏȝt-wisnesse
Miȝte not suffre I leue, ẏ-wisse, 2092
Þat þe cofre worm-ete shulde be
Þat he putte inne his sone so fre,
Þou hure bodẏ were of erthe wrouȝt, fol. 83 a.
Al-þeẏ to erþe turned it nouȝt, 2096
Of oure kẏnde þat is þe lawe ;
Out of such kẏnde sho was ẏ-drawe.
Oure kẏnde askeþ it also,
Womman to beron hure child with wo. 2100
Aȝeẏn kẏnde sho bar with blis ;
Also with bodẏ in heuene sho is.
Maide þat art Cristes gardẏn
And Cristes premerole wexinge þer-in, 2104
Hou mẏȝte þat orchard so swete
Tornen in-to wermes mete.
Maide, þou slest þo dragon Lady, thou hast slain Eve's beguiler.
Þat broȝte mankẏnde in-to prison. 2108
He ouercam womman with gẏle ;
Now haþ womman ẏ-quẏt hẏm his while.
Þou art broȝt, ladẏ, to blisse
Of wich þou mẏȝt neuere mẏsse ; 2112
Þi ioẏe maẏ no tonge telle
Þat þou shalt inne for euer dwelle.
2079. *I* not in MS.

56 Meditations on the Life and Passion of Christ

<small>Angels and saints kneel before thee.</small>

Angels and holẏ soules alle
Doun to þe on knes þeẏ falle ; 2116
Vche is redẏ on his wise
To profre to þe his seruise.
In erþe wex þer neuere flour
Þat mẏȝte be lẏk to þi colour. 2120

<small>Thy beauty is beyond comparison.</small>

Ladẏ, þou art so brẏȝt of ble
Noþẏng likeneþ þi beute.

<small>fol. 88 b.</small>

Primerole to þe is not of pris ;
Þou art rodier þan rose on rẏs. 2124
Þe violet ne lilies clere
Of beute is not þi pere ;
Þe medwes grene and blosmes on tre
Ben in no reward vn-to þe ; 2128
Ne flour in feld on someres-daẏ
Ne lef on tre, ne sprẏng on spraẏ,
Maẏ ben lich þi swete face
Þat is so faẏr and ful of grace. 2132
ffairnesse of flour is sone agon,
Þi beute lesteþ euere in on.

<small>But thy worthiness is greater still.</small>

Ladi, ful muchel is þi fairnesse
And wel more is þi wordẏnesse ; 2136
ffor holẏ writ wiþouten gẏle
Likneþ þe to þe berẏle.
Whan þe berẏle receẏueþ lẏȝt,
And hete of sunne shẏneþ brẏȝt, 2140
So sone as it haþ hete ẏ-wonne
It brenneþ þorw mẏȝt of þe sunne ;
Riȝt so dost þou, mẏ ladẏ swete,
Whan Gabriel þe cam to grete : 2144
Þou conseẏuedest þe sone of rẏȝt
And in loue brendest ful brẏȝt,
Þat diamand is not so dere,
Charbokel shineþ not so clere, 2148
The saphir ne þe amatite,
Topace ne þe cresolẏte ;

<small>fol. 85 a.</small>
<small>All bright things are dark in comparison with thee.</small>

Sunne and mone and sterres brẏȝt
Wexon derke al in þẏ sẏȝt, 2152
Þi face is so ful of beaute
Þat no þing maẏ ben lẏch to þe.

Meditations on the Life and Passion of Christ

Ȝif þo þat be in penaunce dyȝt
Miȝton ones haue of þe a syȝt,   2156
Mikel likyng were to ham lent,
ffor al hure wo were a-wey went.
Lady, suffyse may y noȝt
Wiþ word, with dede, ne with þoȝt,   2160
To preyse þe al as I sholde;
ffor ȝif I myȝt, lady, I wolde.
Louely lady, so koupe y-kud,   *Lady, thou hast bound*
Þe victory þou hast y-hud,   2164 *Christ to thy will.*
And bounden him al at þi wille
And in þi barm he liþ ful stille.
He þat is so strong and sterne,
He may þe noþing werne;   2168
Þei þou him bynde on sw[i]ch manere
He granteþ þe al þy prayere,
And at þy swete comaundement
He wol relese his iuggement.   2172
Þerfore, lady, we praye to þe   *Then plead for us at the Day of Doom.*
Oure help to him þat þou wolt be.
ffor at þat ilke dredful stour
Þou alone art oure socour;   2176
Other help can we non se
But vnder þi wynge for to fle.
Þorw myȝt of þin holy name   *fol. 85 b.*
ffendes fledde a-way with shame;   2180
Þei quaked as dede þe lef on tre
Whan þei herde þe name of þe.
Therefore, þou þat art so swete,
Alle bales þou myȝt bete.   2184
Be in oure mouþ at oure deþ-day,
Þat felle fendes flen away.
Louely lady, maydon of myȝt,
Set in oure myschef þy syȝt.   2188
We ben in foule flesch by-loke,   *We are locked in foul flesh.*
Help oure bondes weron to-broke.
Haue reward to oure trauayle;
We arn by-set with strong batayle   2192

2169. MS. *swch.*

> Wiþ world and flesch and fendes felle;
> Oure wo maẏ no tonge telle;
> And of oure-selue we arn not strong
> To suffre þis trauaile long; 2196
> ffor we ben faẏnter þan þe flour
> Þat with þe wẏnd leseþ his colour.

Of ourselves we have no might.
> Of oure-self haue we no mẏȝt
> Wẏþ oure fomen for to fẏȝt; 2200
> ffor oure kẏnde is more for-feẏnt
> Þan asshen ben whan fir is queẏnt.
> We vanẏschon a[s] smoke a-waẏ
> And welke as floures in wẏnter daẏ. 2204
> We tornon al to wormes ware;
> Out of þis world we wendon bare,

fol. 87 a.
> Þus ben we wiþ wo bẏ-set;
> Wiþ muche mornẏng we han met. 2208
> Oure lẏf is ful of sẏknesse,
> Oure deþ is ful of wrecchednesse.
> Siknesse and deþ resteþ noȝt
> Til erþe be tẏl erþe brouȝt. 2212
> Þanne haue wermes al hure wille
> To fedon hem with flesch hure fille.
> Soreẏ maẏ þanne man be
> But ȝif his saule be more fre 2216
> Þan þat foule carful careẏne
> Þat wermes haue in hure demaẏne.
> Þerfore, moder of mercẏ,
> Herkene to oure carful crẏ; 2220

Our trust is in thee alone.
> ffor al oure trust on þe is lent,
> And but þou helpe, we ben ẏ-shent.
> On þe is al oure trust ẏ-set;
> Þou most ben oure a-voket, 2224
> At þe dredful domes-daẏ
> Help vs, ladẏ, as þou wel maẏ.
> Whan þi sone sit on his se
> Wiþ woundes as he died on tre, 2228
> ffor to deme vs alle ful blẏue
> After oure desert in oure lẏue,

2203. MS. *a.*

Þanne, lady, praẏe for vs
To þi sone, swete Ihesus,   2232   Plead our cause before thy Son.
In þat ilke carful cas,
þat he for-ȝẏue vs oure trespas.
Ȝif he be hard to for-ȝẏue   fol. 87 b.
And graunte grace þat we may lẏue,   2236
Preẏ hym for þat ilke loue
Þat drow him doun from heuene aboue
To souke of þi swete tete,
Þat he wolde oure peẏnes bete;   2240
ffor oure sẏnne al-þeẏ it be sterne,
Þin askẏng wil he þe not werne.
Opẏn, lady, þis ilke bok   Open before him this book of praising.
Bẏfore him þat oure kẏnde tok,   2244
Þat for þis preẏsẏng sake
Somdel he wole oure serwes slake.
And now, moder and maẏdon swete,
Wiþ þis preẏsẏng I þe grete;   2248   With it I greet thee.
And alle þat hauon þis in mẏnde,
Kẏndam in heuene þou shalt hem sende.
Worshipe, blis, and praẏsẏng
Aẏ be to þe, heuene kẏng;   2252
Loue and ioẏe and gret lẏkẏng,
Godes sone wiþouten gẏnnẏng.

Amen.

APPENDIX

AN ORISON OF THE PASSION

THE text of the *Orison* is printed from MS. Bodl. Add. E. 4 with variant readings from MS. Bodley 850 (B), and MS. e Mus. 232 (E). In vv. 9, 10 and 12 where the writing has been rubbed, the missing letters are supplied in brackets from readings common to the other MSS. Alterations in the MS. reading are put in in brackets, and the MS. reading is noted below. The numbering on the left refers to the corresponding lines in the *Meditations*. Lines marked with an asterisk are those not used in the *Meditations*. Punctuation has been supplied by the editor.

MS. Bodl. Add. E. 4.

AN ORISON OF THE PASSION

IN seyinge of þis orisone stinteþ *and* abideþ[1] at euery crose and þinkeþ whate ȝe haue seide; ffor a more deuout prayer fonde y neuer of þe passione, who-so wolde abidingly[2] sey it.[3]

  *Ihesu þat haste me der a-bouȝte,
  *Write þou[4] gostly in my þouȝte
  *þat y mow wiþ deuocioune
  *Þinke vpon[5] þi passione.   4
1355 for þouȝ myn herte be harde as stone,
  Ȝite maiste þou gostly write þer-one
  Wiþ naylis and wiþ sper kene,
1358 And so schulen þe lettres be wel[6] sene.   8
1371 Write in myne herte wiþ[7] spechis swete
  Whane Iudas þe traytour gan [þe m]ete;
  Þat traytour was full of þe fende,
1374 And ȝit þou calle[dest hym] þi frende.   12
1399 Swet Ihesu, how myȝte þou so
  Callen[8] þi frende so felle a[9] foo.

[1] bydeth E.   [2] deuoutly E.   [3] as hit folweth *added* E.
[4] nowe B.   [5] on þy der p. E.   [6] *put after* shall B; *omitted* E.
[7] þi B.   [8] cal hym E.   [9] *and* E.

60

An Orison of the Passion

	But sepẏn þou spake so louelẏ	
	To him þat was þin enemẏ,	16
	How swete schule þi spechis be	
1404	To heme þat hertly louen þe,	
	*Whane þei in heuen wiþ þe schule dwellen;	
	*I-wys, þer may no tonge tellen.	20
1375	Write how þu wer bounden sore	
	And drawen forþ Pilate bifore;	
	And [1] how swetly þou answerde þoo	
1378	To him þat was þi felle foo.	24
1411	Write how þat false [2] enqueste	
	Cried ay wiþ-outen reste,	
	"Honge him on þe roode tre,	
1414	ffor he wille [3] kinge of Iewis be."	28
	Write vpone mẏne herte booke	
	Þi fayre and swete loueli [4] looke,	
	ffor schame of her hẏdous crẏe	
1418	Þat wolden of þe haue no mercy.	32
1423	Write how whane þe crose was forþ broȝte	
	And þe nayles of yrne wrouȝte,	
	[Þ] [5] ou ganne [6] to cheueren and quake;	
1426	Þin herte was wo, þouȝ þou noȝte [7] spake.	36
	Write hou downewarde þou gane lokene	
	Whane Iewus to þe þe crose [8] betokene;	
	Þou bare it forþ wiþ rewly chere,	
1430	Þe [9] teeres ronnen downe to [10] þi lere.	40
1359	Ihesu, write in mẏne herte deepe,	
	how þat þou be-ganne to wepe,[11]	
	Þo [12] þi backe was to þe roode y bente,	
1362	Wiþ rugged naẏles þine hondes rente.	44
	Write þe strokes of [13] hamers stoute	
	Wiþ þe [14] bloode rennẏnge aboute;	
	how þe naẏlis stẏnten at þe bone;	
1366	Whan þou wer fule wo-bigone.	48
1483	Ihesu, ȝite write in mẏne herte	
	How bloode oute of þi wondis sterte;	
	And wiþ þat [15] bloode write þow so ofte	
1486	Mẏne harde herte tile hit be softe.	52

[1] omitted B. [2] fell B. [3] wolde B. [4] rulẏ B. [5] hou MS.
[6] began BE. [7] ne E. [8] þe to þe crosse B. [9] and B. [10] bi BE.
[11] swete E. [12] when B. [13] with E. [14] þi B. [15] þi B.

1349	Ihesu þat arte so mokel of mýȝte,	
	Write in mýne herte þat rewfule siȝte	
	To loken¹ on þi moder free	
1352	Whane þou were honged one² þe roode tre.	56
1455	Write³ þi swete modres woo	
	Whane sche sawȝ þe to deþ goo;	
	I-wys, þouȝ y write alle mý lyue	
1458	I schulde neuer hir wo discrýue.	60
1335	In mýne herte aẏ mote it be,	
	Þat harde knottẏ roode tree;	
	The naylis and þe spere also	
1338	Þat þou wer wiþ⁴ to deþ y-do;	64
	Þe corowne and þe scowrges grete	
	Þat þou wer wiþ so sore ẏbete;	
	Thi wepinge and⁵ þi woundis wýde,	
1342	Þe bloode þat ranne downe bi þi syde,	68
	The schame, þe scorne, and⁶ þe⁷ gret despite,	
	Þe spotile þat fouled þi face white,⁸	
	Þe eysil and þe bittyr galle,	
	And oþer of þi peynes alle.	72
	ffor while ẏ haue hem in mý thouȝte	
1348	Þe deuyl ẏ hope schale der me noȝte.	
1503	Ihesu, write þus⁹ þat ẏ mote know	
	how mokel loue to þe ẏ owe;	76
	ffor þouȝ þat ẏ wil fro þe flee	
1506	Þou folowiste aẏ to saue me.	
1425	Ihesu, whane ẏ thinke on þe,	
	how þou wer bounde for loue of me,	80
	Wel owe ẏ to wepe þat stounde	
	Þat þou for me so¹⁰ sore wer bounde.	
	But þou þat bare vpon þin hondis	
	ffor mý sýnne¹¹ so bittýr bondis	84
	wiþ¹² loue-bondis¹² binde þou so me	
1432	Þat y neuer be departed fro þe.	
2019	Ihesu þat wer wiþ loue so bounde,	
	Þat¹³ suffred for me deþ-wounde,	88

---

¹ Whenn þou loked B.   ² The tyme þou hing vpon B.
³ vv. 57–62 *omitted* B.   ⁴ Wher-with þou were B.   ⁵ *omitted* B.
⁶ *omitted* E.   ⁷ *omitted* B.   ⁸ so white E.   ⁹ þis E.   ¹⁰ *omitted* B.
¹¹ loue B; synnes E.   ¹² *phrase omitted* B.   ¹³ thowe *added* B.

An Orison of the Passion

	At my deyinge so [1] visite me	
2022	And make þe fende a-way to fle.	
1331	Ihesu, make me gladde to be	
	Symple and pore for loue of þe,	92
	And lete me neuer for more [n]e [2] lesse	
1334	louen goode to mokel þat sone schale passe.	
1677	Ihesu þat arte kinge of lyfe,	
1678	Teche my soule þat is þi wyfe [3]	96
1681	To louen beste no þinge [4] in londe	
	Bute þe, Ihesu, [5] here der hosbande.	
	ffor oþur blisse and oþer bewte	
	Be hit foule and sorow to se;	100
1685	ffor oþer ioy and oþer blisse	
	wo and sorow for soþ it is,	
	And lesteþ but a litel while	
1688	Mannes soule for [6] to be-gýle.	104
1625	Ihesu, [7] late me fele whate ioy it be	
	To suffren wo for loue of þe;	
	Hou mery it is for [þe] [8] to weep,	
	How softe it is [9] in harde cloþes to slepe.	108
1629	Let now loue his bowe benden	
	And loue arowis to mýne herte senden,	
	Thate y [10] mow perschene to [11] þe roote,	
1632	ffor swiche woundis [12] schule be my boote.	112
1609	Whane y am low for þi loue,	
	Þane ame y moste at mýne a-boue;	
	ffastinge is feste, mornynge is blise,	
	ffor þi loue pouert is richesse.	116
1613	Þe [13] harde heýre schale [14] be more of prise	
	Þan softe silke or pelure or býse.	
	Defaute for þi loue is plente	
	And fleschli luste wel [15] loþ schulde be.	120
1617	Whane y ame wiþ wo bistade	
	ffor þi loue þan ame y glade.	
	To suffre scornes and grete despite	
1620	ffor loue of þe is my delite.	124

[1] þou B.   [2] me MS.   [3] wyfe *omitted* B.
[4] To loue þi best of thinge B.   [5] Bute þe, *omitted*, Swete ihesu B.
[6] *omitted* B.   [7] *omitted* B.   [8] *omitted in MS. and* E.
[9] it is *omitted* B.   [10] thei B; hit E.   [11] *omitted* B.   [12] a wounde B.
[13] This B.   [14] schale *written twice* MS.   [15] full B.

1633	Ihesu, mak me ofte ¹ to wake	
	And in my þou3te þi name to take;	
	And wheþer þe ny3te be schorte or longe	
	Of þe, Ihesu, ay ² mote be ² mÿ songe.	128
1637	Late þis prayer a cheÿne be	
	To drawe þe downe of ³ þi see,	
	Þat ẏ mow make þe a dwellinge	
1640	In mÿne herte at þi lÿkinge.	132
1225	Ihesu, y praẏe ⁴ for-sake no3t me	
	Þou3 y of synne gilty be;	
	ffor to ⁵ p.it þef þat henge þe bi	
	Redilẏ þou 3afe hÿme þi mercẏ	136
1229	Ihesu, þat grete cortesÿe ⁶	
	Mekeþ ⁷ me bolde on þe to crẏe;	
	ffor wel ẏ wote wiþ-outen drede	
1232	Þi mercy is more þane mÿ mÿsdede.	140
2027	Ihesu þat arte so lefe and dere,	
	Hẏre and spede þis pore prayer.	
Dorso of MS.	ffor Poule þat was so felle and woode	
	To spilen Cristen mennes bloode,	144
2031	To þe wolde he no prayer make	
	And ⁸ 3itte ⁹ þou woldeste him note forsake.	
	Þan mayste þou no3te forsaken me	
	Seþen þat ẏ preẏ þus to þe.	148
2035	At mẏ dyinge y hope, ẏ-wẏs,¹⁰	
	Of þi presence schale ẏ no3te mys.	
	Ihesu, make me þan to rẏse	
	frome deþ to lyue on suche a wyse	152
	As þou rose vpe on Estyr daye	
2040	In ioye and blisse to lyuen ¹¹ aye.	
	Amen.	

¹ a-ny3t BE.   ² be euer E.   ³ oute of B.   ⁴ þe *added* BE.
⁵ *omitted* E.   ⁶ þat art so corteisly E.   ⁷ make E.   ⁸ *omitted* B.
⁹ *omitted* E.   ¹⁰ *verse omitted* B.   ¹¹ haue B.

INDEX OF PROPER NAMES

ABEL, 1260 ; *gen.* Abeles, 1261
Adam, 411, 1566, 1567, 1569 ; *gen.*
    Adamis, 1253 ; new Adam=Christ,
    1254
Ambros, St. Ambroise, 1967
Archangels, an order of angels, 1117
Aungels, an order of angels, 1118
Austyn, St. Augustine, 1993
Baraban, Barabas, 515, 1439
Bernard, St. Bernard, 1967
Caluery, 1562
Caym, Cain, 1260
Cherubyn, an order of angels, 1103
Clement, bishop of Rome, 1947
Crist, 167, 412, 580, 710, etc.
Dauid, King David, 118, 1272 ; *gen.*
    Dauides, 9
Dionys, Dionysius the Areopagite ?
    1967
Domenik, St. Dominic, founder of the
    Dominican order, 1985
Domynacyoun, an order of angels,
    1110
Esterday, Easterday, 2039
Fraunceis, St. Francis of Assisi, 1989
Gabriel, archangel, 2144
God, 182, 655, etc.; Godes (*gen.*), 896
Gregor, St. Gregory, 1967
Heroud, Hero(u)des, 135, 504, 506,
    1403
Iacob, 711
Ierom, St. Jerome, 1963
Iewes, Jews, 488, 542, 656, 840, 992,
    1428, etc.
Ihesu(s), 768, 775, 779, 1075, etc.
Innocentes, the Innocents, 136
Iob, 1267, 1703, 1705, 1709

Iohan, Ion, St. John the Evangelist,
    1220, 1951, 1966
Iosep, Joseph the patriarch, 1255
Iudas, 389, 393, 397
Iulius Cesar, 983
Kateryne, St. Catherine, 1975
Laurence, St. Laurence, 1955
La3er, Lazarus, 218
Machabeus, 1269
Magdelayn, see under Marie Magde-
    leyn
Margarete, St. Margaret, 1977
Marie Magdeleyn, 2046 ; Magdelayn,
    fed from heaven, 1979 ; Maude-
    leynes (*gen.*), sister of Lazarus, 209
Marye, the Virgin, 1173, 1221, 1871
May, the month, 753, 1277, 1469,
    1900.
Noe, Noah, 193, 715
Olyuet, Mt. Olivet, 366
Paul(e), St. Paul, 1045, 1953, 2029
Petre(er), St. Peter, 441, 1049, 1943
Pilat(e), Pylat, 492, 496, 501, 509, 1376,
    etc.
Potestates, an order of angels, 1113
Saul, King Saul, 1271
Seraphyn, an order of angels, 1101
Steuene, St. Stephen, 1939
Symeon, high-priest, 177
Thomas, St. Thomas the apostle, 2062
Thomas, archbishop of Canterbury,
    1971
Trouns, Thrones, an order of angels,
    1105
Virtutes, an order of angels, 1111
Vyncent, St. Vincent, 1959
Ysaye, Isaiah, 498

GLOSSARY

The glossary includes only the more important words with their variant spellings. The following abbreviations are used: *a.*, adjective; *adv.*, adverb; *art.*, article; *comp.*, comparative; *dat.*, dative; *def.*, definite; *gen.*, genitive; *imper.*, imperative mood; *imperson.*, impersonal; *negat.*, negative; *num.*, numeral; *obj.*, objective case, dative or accusative; *pl.*, plural; *poss.*, possessive; *pp.*, past participle; *pr.*, present tense; *pr. pt.*, present participle; *pret.*, preterite tense; *pron.*, pronoun; *s.*, substantive; *sing.*, singular; *v.*, verb.

A

ABAY, *s.*, *in phrase* at bay, to bay, 450
a-bere, *adv. phrase*, on bier, 838
a-bobbedon, *pret.* 3 *pl.*, struck, 1512
a-bobbynge, *s.*, striking, 1402
aboute, *adv.*, about, around, 906, 1364
abo3te, *pret.* 3 *sing.*, paid for, 1565; *pp.*, abo3t, 798
abrod, *adv.*, abroad, 343, 1827
abydon, *v.*, to abide, await, 1444
abydyng, *s.*, abiding, 824.
acorde, *v.*, to agree, 1989
acursed, *pp.*, 1514
acuseth, *pr.* 3 *sing.*, accuses, 479; *pp.*, acused, 494
adoun, *adv.*, down, 169, 318, 1028
afore, aforn, *adv.*, before, formerly, 1446, 1756
aforn, *prep.*, before, 141
afray, *s.*, assault, 1705, 1974
after, *adv. and prep.*, 21; for, 31, 833; according to, 213
agast, *pp.*, aghast, 224
agon, *pp.*, gone, 178, 2133
almy3ty, *a.*, almighty, 448
also, *adv.*, also, besides, 53, 84; thus, similarly, 202, 271; also swyde, immediately, 1582
al-þey, *conj.*, although, 1133, 1209, 1226

al-þey, *adv.*, nevertheless, 2096
a-lyue, *adv.*, alive, 522; *see* on lyue *under* lif.
amatite, *s.*, amethyst, 2149
amende, *v.*, to amend, 694
among, *adv.*, at the same time, 172, 601, 1080
among, amonges, *prep.*, among, in the midst of, 603, 2072
amys, *adv.*, amiss, 447, 2056
an, *prep.*, on, 1217
and, *conj.*, if, 332, 569, 1129
angel, aungel, *s.*, 382, 1103; *gen.*, angeles, 44, 125
anon, *adv.*, at once, 285, 296
answerede, *pret.* 3 *sing.*, answered, 1377
any, *s.*, annoyance, 386
a-ny3t, *adv.*, at night, 1013, 1633
apere, *v.*, to appear, 2047
apostel(le), *s.*, 441, 1953; *pl.*, aposteles, 2052.
appel-tre, *s.*, 1569
aqueynt, *pp.*, quenched, 1950; *for* adreynt ? 1949
archebischop, *s.*, 1971
arise, *pret.* 2 *sing.*, arose, 2039; *pp.*, arise, 2045
armure, *s.*, armor, 1586, 1595
arwe, *s.*, arrow, 1630
ary3t, *adv.*, rightly, 891, 1533
as(s)aile, *v.*, to assail, 120, 240

Glossary.

asay, *s.*, essay, trial, 1581
ascryedon, *pret.* 3 *pl.*, cried out upon, 1454
askeþ, *pr.* 3 *sing.*, asks, 2057, 2099; *pr.* 3 *pl.*, askon, 1126; *pret.* 3 *sing. and pl.*, asked, 776, 1749
askyng, *s.*, request, 2242
a-slepe, *adv.*, asleep, 156
asper, *a.*, sharp, 238
asse, *s.*, ass, 1597; *gen.*, asse, 1318
assentedon, *pret.* 3 *pl.*, assented, 1481
asshen, *s.*, ashes, 2202
at, *prep.*, according to, 4, 57
ate, *prep.*, at the, 1302
a-þurst, *used as adj.*, athirst, 1576, 1781
auȝte, *pret.* 1 & 3 *sing.*, ought, 423, 1795; 2 *sing.*, auȝtest, 785
avayle, *v.*, to avail, 664
avoket, *s.*, advocate, 2224.
awake, *subj. pr.* 3 *sing.*, 1644
awreke, *pp.*, avenged, 542
aȝeyn, *conj.*, at the time, when, 491
aȝeyn, *adv.*, again, 94, 296; aȝen, 306
aȝeyne(s), *prep.*, against, 478, 1598

B

bak, *s.*, back, 1138, 1361, 1550
bale, *s.*, bale, distress, 322, 1866; *pl.*, bales, 912, 1094
bauer, *s.*, banner, 699, 701, 1604
banned, *pp.*, 42
barm, *s.*, bosom, 29, 145
barres, *s.*, bars, 829
bataile, batayle, *s.*, 119, 239
bay, *s., in phrase*, to bay, 1759; *see* abay.
be, bee, ben, *v.*, to be, 4, 280, 282; *pr.* 1 *sing.*, am, 339; 2 *sing.*, art, 69, 96; 3 *sing.*, is, 28, 33; 1 *pl.*, arn, 2192, 2 *pl.*, be, 310; ben, 340; 3 *pl.* arn, 75; ben, 116, 119; *pret.* 2 *sing.*, were, 13, 15; was, 292; 3 *sing.*, was, 21, 27; 1 *pl.*, weron, 1002; 3 *pl.*, weron, 97, 190; were, 143, 172; *subj. pr.* 1 *sing.*, be, 807; 3 *sing.*, be, 320, 677; *pret.* 1 *sing.*, were, 1161; 3 *sing.*, were, 529; *imper. sing.*, be, 1, 224; *pl.*, beþ, 305; *pp.*, ben, 147, 288; *negat. pr.* 1 *sing.*, nam, 1731; 3 *sing.*, nis, nys, 1172, 1259; *phrases*, to be(n) at þin (his, myn) aboue, to have the advantage, 674, 1330, 1610
be, *prep.*, by, 756
beaute, beute, *s.*, 1197, 2122
bee, *s.*, 1669
begyle, *v.*, to beguile, 1688
begynneþ, *pr.* 3 *sing.*, begins, 645, 1122; 1 *pl.*, bygynne, 1004; *pret.* 3 *sing.*, began, 491; 3 *pl.*, bygonnon, 359; bigonne, 617
behynde, *prep.*, 1292
benam, *pret.* 3 *sing.*, took away, 922
ber(e), *s.*, bier, 746, 860, 1162
bere, beron, *v.*, to bear, 748, 986; *pr.* 1 *sing.*, bere, 1691, 1693; 2 *sing.*, berest, 91, 429; 3 *sing.*, bereth, 478, 631; 3 *pl.*, beren, 1969; *pret.* 2 *sing.*, bere, 683; 3 *sing.*, bar, 557, 753, 2101; 3 *pl.*, beron, 503; *pr. pt.*, beryng, 1552; *pp.*, bore, 360; born, 25, 78; y-born, 129
bernynge, *pr. pt.*, *see under* brenneþ
beryle, *s.*, beryl, 2138, 2139
beset, byset, *pp.*, beset, filled, 14, 1470, 2016
beseyn, *pp.*, covered, overwhelmed, 1747
beshut, *pp.*, shut in, locked, 1932
bestad, bystad, *pp.*, set about, fixed, 1202, 1617, 1774
bet, *adv.*, better, 888
bete, beton, *v.*, to beat, 528, 606; *pr.* 3 *pl.*, beton, 1728; *pp.*, bete, 462, 529; i(y)-bete, 634, 1340; beton, 1501
bettre, *a.*, better, 696
bidde, *pr.* 1 *sing.*, bid, 1701; *pret.* 2 *sing.*, bad, 270, 2062; 3 *sing.*, bad, 1986; 3 *pl.*, beden, 1580
biried, *pp.*, buried, 216
bitter, *a.*, better, 1168
bitter, bytter, *a.*, bitter, harsh, 412, 561, 1307
blak, *a.*, black, 752, 1020, 1311
ble, *s.*, color, 997, 1181, 2121
blede, *v.*, to bleed, 1034, 1501; *pr.* 3 *sing.*, blet, 418, 573; *pret.* 3 *pl.*, bledon, 1877
blent, *pp.*, blended, 910.

blesse, *v.*, to bless, 563; *pr.* 1 *pl.*,
    blesse, 25; *pp.*, blessed, 1057; *used
    as a.*, 48
bliech, *a.*, colourless, pale, 641
blo(o), *a.*, blue, 641, 752, 1020
blod(e), *s.*, blood, 136, 1436; *gen.*,
    blodes, 635
blome, *s.*, bloom, 720
blosme, *s.*, blossom, 1922; *pl.*, blosmes, 2127
blyue, *adv.*, quickly, 2046, 2229; *also*
    blyue, at once, 521
bobbed, *pp.*, struck, 459; *see* a-bobbedon.
bodely, *adv.*, in the flesh, 1906
bok, *s.*, book, 884, 2243
bon, *s.*, bone, 286, 887
bonde-lord, *s.*, a lord in the position of
    a bond-servant, 1312.
bone, *s.*, boon, 1701
bosom, *s.*, 105; *dat.*, bosme, 103
bote, *s.*, help, 1061, 1632
boundes, *s.*, bounds, 2059
bounte, *s.*, bounty, goodness, 128, 648
bouȝt, *pp.*, bought, 956
bow, *s.*, bough, 842
bowe, *s.*, bow, 1629
brak, *pret.* 3 *sing.*, broke, 1842; *imper.
    sing.*, brek, 830; *pp.*, broke, 1009;
    broken, 232, 2042
bred, *s.*, bread, *in the phrase* bred of
    lyf, *applied to Christ*, 114, 124, 817
brede, *v.*, to breed, 708
breme, *a.*, sharp (of thorns), 548
brengon, *v.*, *see under* bryngon
brenneþ, *pr.* 3 *sing.*, burns, 870, 1301,
    2142; *pret.* 2 *sing.*, brendest, 2146;
    pr. pl., brennyng(e), 802, 1075, 1102;
    bernynge, 1314; brennend, 1958;
    pp., brent, 898
brennyng, *s.*, burning, 1322
brere, *s.*, briar, 561
brere-tre, *s.*, thorn, 572
brest(e), *s.*, breast, 48, 87
breste, *v.*, to burst, 1145, 1354
briddes, *s.*, (young) birds, 1280; *gen.*,
    briddes, 694
briȝt, bryȝt(e), *a.*, 166, 1592, 1840;
    brigthe, 146; bryȝtest, 1834

brode, *a.*, broad, 64
brode, *adv.*, broadly, 1198
brother, *s.*, 209, 1260; *pl.*, breþeren,
    1725, 1986; brederen, 1256
brunye, *s.*, byrnie, coat of mail, 1591
brymston, *s.*, 1320
bryng(e), bryngon, *v.*, to bring, 180,
    492, 714, 1012; brengon, 746; *pr.*
    2 *sing.*, brengest, 848; 3 *sing.*,
    bryngeþ, 1120; 3 *pl.*, brengon, 1257;
    pret. 2 *sing.*, broughtest, 608; 3
    sing., brogthe, 247; broȝte, 2108;
    pp., brouȝt, 450, 509; broȝt, 786,
    1423
burde, *s.*, maiden, 166
but, *adv.*, only, 593, 1687
but, *conj.*, unless, 826, 1347; but ȝif,
    unless, 2216
but, *prep.*, except, 112, 215, 1172;
    without, 291
by, *prep.*, by, along, 541, 1430
by-bled, *pp.*, covered with blood, 1858
byclipped, *MS. reading for* byclippen,
    v., to embrace, 1828
bycomeþ, *pr.* 3 *sing.*, becomes, is fitting, 736; *pret.* 2 *sing.*, bycome,
    became, 2
bydene, *adv.*, all together, 635
byfalle, *v.*, to befall, 2002; *subj. pr.*
    3 *sing.*, byfalle, 218
byforon, *prep.*, before, 504
bygon, *pp.*, covered, overspread, 575,
    1319, 2015
byhold, *imper. sing.*, 577, 1707; *subj.
    pr.* 3 *sing.*, byholde, 1030
byleue, *s.*, belief, faith, 59
byleuon, *v.*, to believe, 2065; *pr.* 1
    sing., byleue, 2079
byloke, *pp.*, locked, imprisoned, 655,
    1255, 2189
bynt, *pr.* 3 *sing.*, binds, 1224; *pr.* 2
    pl., bynde, 413; *pret.* 3 *sing.*, bond,
    1825; *subj. pr.* 2 *sing.*, bynde, 2169;
    imper. sing., bynd, 431; *pp.*, bounde,
    24, 1717; ybounde, 433, 813; bounden, 426, 1885; bondon, 406
byronne, *pp.*, overrun, 963
byrthe, *s.*, birth, 18
bysmare, *s.*, scorn, derision, 614

Glossary. 69

byspat, *pp.*, spit upon, 1396
bytok(e)neþ, *pr.* 3 *sing.*, betokens, 1706, 1991
bywake, *pp.*, watched, guarded, 1744

C

can, *pr.* 1 *sing.*, know, am able, 1538, 2082; 3 *sing.*, can, 473, 587; *pret.* 3 *sing.*, koude, 618; coude, 1763; 3 *pl.*, coude, 1748; *pp.*, ykud, 2163
careyne, *see under* caroyne.
caroyne, *s.*, flesh, body, 1286; careyne, 2217
carful, *a.*, sorrowful, 229, 368, 2217
carpe, *s.*, discourse, 1069
cas, *s.*, case, situation, 381, 446
cast, *pr.*, 2 *sing.*, cast, cast off, 927; *pret.* 3 *sing.*, cast, 1398; *pp.*, cast, 318, 1831
cauth, *pp.*, caught, 26
caytyf, *s.*, wretch, outcast, 818; *pl.*, caytyfs, 453
chaf, *s.*, chaff, straw, 1837
chanyeth, *pr.* 3 *sing.*, changes, 1746
chapelet, *s.*, chaplet, 539
charbokel, *s.*, carbuncle, 2148
charied, *pp.*, charged, weighted, 989
charyte, *s.*, charity, 652
chaumpioun, *s.*, 643
cheke, *s.*, 451, 541; *pl.*, chekes, 115, 476
cherche, *s.*, *gen.*, church's, 707
chere, *s.*, countenance, 368, 866
cheualry, *s.*, 1856
cheyne, *s.*, chain, 1637; *pl.*, cheynes, 233
chyn, *s.*, 451
chyuere, *v.*, to shiver, 1425
clater, *v.*, to clatter, to shake to pieces, 486
clene, *a.*, clean, pure, 16, 312, 1642
clense, *v.*, to cleanse, 196; *pr.* 3 *sing.*, clenseþ, 1088
clepe, *v.*, to call, 400; *pr.* 1 *sing.*, clepe, 314; 3 *pl.*, clepon, 543; *pret.* 3 *sing.*, clepede, 1374; 3 *pl.*, clepedon, 594, 1410; *subj. pr.* 2 *sing.*, clepe, 1209; *pp.*, ycleped, 1105; cleped, 1303

cleue, *v.*, to cleave, 486; *pp.*, ycleft, 2011
clere, *adv.*, clearly, 2148
clipte, *see under* cluppe
clodeþ, *pret.* 3 *sing. for* cloþed, 1385; *pret.* 3 *sing.*, cloþed, 1403; clodeþ, *for* cloþed, 940
cloþ, *s.*, 1382, 1761; *pl.*, cloþes, 964, 1407
cluppe, *v.*, to embrace, 1908; *pret.* 3 *sing.*, clipte, 153, 1778
cluppyng, *s.*, embracing, 1645
cofre, *s.*, coffer, 2093
colded, *pret.* 3 *sing.*, grew cold, 1502
coluer, *see under* culuer
comandest, *pr.* 2 *sing.*, 815; 3 *sing.*, comaundeþ, 1819
come, comen, comon, *v.*, 296, 663, 1906; *pr.* 1 *sing.*, come, 306; 2 *sing.*, comes, 398; 3 *sing.*, cometh, 389, 419; 3 *pl.*, comon, 1112, 1117; *pret.* 2 *sing.*, com, 2067; 3 *sing.*, cam, 46, 60; com, 254; 3 *pl.*, kemon, 140, 535, 1475; *subj. pr.* 3 *sing.*, come, 1910; *imper. sing.*, com, 218, 224; *pp.*, comon, 143
comely, *a.*, 1646
compenye, *s.*, company, following, 229, 1115
confort, *s.*, comfort, 1085
conseyuedest, *pret.* 2 *sing.*, conceived, 17, 2145
continaunce, *s.*, assurance, composure, 618
corde, *s.*, cord worn by a friar, 1990
corn, *s.*, grain, 113
cornel, *s.*, kernel, 721
corone, *s.*, crown, 1339, 1602; corun, 818; *pl.*, corones, 556
corone, *v.*, to crown, 546, 561; *pr.* 3 *sing.*, crouneþ, 878; *pret.* 3 *pl.*, corondon, 544; korendon, 536; *pp.*, coronet, 1026
coronement, *s.*, coronation, 553, 1367
coronyng, *s.*, crowning, 570
corrupcyoun, *s.*, decay, 2086
corteys, *see under* curteys
corun, *see under* corone
cote, *s.*, coat, 939, 1258

coude, koude, *see under* can
coueityse, *s.*, covetousness, 1473
couere, *imper. sing.*, cover, 665
counsail, counseyl, *s.*, counsel, 1678, 1903
coupe, *see under* cuppe
coupe, *a.*, well-known, 1965
cradel-bond, *s.*, cradle-band, swaddling-band, 24
crestes, *s.*, crests, of a helmet, 1590
cresolyte, *s.*, chrysolite, 2150
cristened, *pp.*, 195
criston, *a.*, Christian, 354
crois, croys, *s.*, 699, 725, 981
crouneþ, *see under* corone, *v.*
crye, *v.*, to cry, 230, 518; *pr. 3 sing.*, crieth, 31; *pret. 3 pl.*, cryedon, 1412
culuer, *s.*, dove, 1316; coluer, 1599
cuppe, *s.*, cup, 36, 881; coupe, 269
ourour, *s.*, courier, 1721
curtesye, *s.*, courtesy, 1229
curteys, *a.*, courteous, 1489; corteys, 287

D

damage, *s.*, injury, 957
damosel, *s.*, 91
dampned, *pret. 3 sing.*, condemned, 1434; *pr. 3 sing.*, dampned *for* dampneþ, 1370
dar, *pr. 3 sing.*, dares, 705
dawe(s), *see under* day
day, *s.*, 50, 491; *gen.*, dayes, 1282; *pl.*, dayes, 211, 1723; of dawe, from life, 944; by olde dawes, in former times, 1736
day-lyȝt, *s.*, daylight, 976
ded, *s.*, *see under* deþ
ded, *a.*, dead, 216, 628, 670; *pl.* dede, 1146
defaute, *s.*, want, 1615
defes, *see under* þef
dele, *s.*, sorrow, 1164
delful, *a.*, doleful, 1144, 1754
delfuly, *adv.*, dolefully, 466
deliueredest, *pret. 2 sing.*, delivered, 516; *pp.*, delyuered, 1934
delys, *s.*, delight, 258, 457
delyt, *s.*; delight, 1620
demaÿne, *s.*, possession, 2218
deme, *v.*, to judge, 2229

departed, *pp.*, parted, 304
depaynt, *pp.*, painted, 623
depe, *adv.*, deeply, 1359
dere, *a.*, dear, 266, 973
dere, *adv.*, dearly, 798, 1565
derk, *a.*, dark, 456; *pl.*, derke, 2152; *comp.*, derker, 920
derlyng, *s.*, darling, 1258
desert, *s.*, merit, 2230
desese, *s.*, discomfort, 173
deþ(o), *s.*, death, 183, 208; *gen.*, deþes, 428, 689; dede, 1456; *gen.*, dedes, 290, 1875
deþ-day, *s.*, day of death, 2185
deuel, *s.*, devil, 206, 717; *gen.*, deueles, 200, 1056
die, dye, *v.*, to die, 744, 1032; dion, 1152; *pr. 3 sing.*, dieþ, 1837; *prɩt. 2 sing.*, deiedest, 1289; *3 sing.*, died, 2228; *pp.*, y-deyd, 755
died, *pp.*, dyed, 370
dilicyous, *a.*, delicious, 43, 101
discomfited, *pp.*, defeated, 72
discomfiture, *s.*, defeat, 253
discyple, *s.*, 1220; *pl.*, disciples, 310, 2067
dispit, dyspyt, *s.*, despite, 507, 1812
displaid, *pp.*, displayed, 703
disport, *s.*, pleasure, 293, 1086
diȝte, *v.*, to prepare, to array, 301; *pp.*, diȝt, dyȝt, 372, 377, 466; y-dyȝt, 1298; dight, dyght, 107, 183, 392
dom, *s.*, judgment, 1447
don, *v.*, to do, to cause, 202; *pr. 1 sing.*, do, 612; *3 sing.*, doth, 162, 166; *2 pl.*, do, 604; *pret. 2 sing.*, dedest, 293; *3 sing.*, dede, 104, 504; *3 pl.*, dedon, 447; *imper. sing.*, do, 512; *pp.*, don, 271, 915; y-don, 532; y-do, 1205, 1338
doubleþ, *pr. 3 sing.*, doubles, 1690
drad, *see under* drede
dragon, *s.*, serpent, 2107
drauȝt, . draught, 881
drawe, *v.*, to draw, to approach, 380, 943; *pret. 3 sing.*, drow, 2238; *3 pl.*, drowen, 1516; *pp.*, drawen, 1021; y-drawe, 251, 2098

Glossary. 71

drede, *v.*, to dread; 1063; *pr.* 1 *sing.*,
drede, 1910; 3 *sing.*, dredeþ, 1984;
3 *pl.*, drede, 991; *pret.* 3 *sing.*,
dredde, 1948, 1976; dradde, 1974,
1982; *pp.*, drad, *as a.*, filled with
dread, 1495
dredful, *a.*, 221, 706, 1500
drieþ, *pr.* 3 *sing.*, dries, 846; *pret.* 2
sing., dreiedest, 193
drinke, drynk, drynkon, *v.*, to drink,
270, 274, 654; *pr.* 2 *sing.*, drynkes,
774, drynkest, 1524; 3 *sing.*, drynk-
eth, 1770; drynged (*for*-eþ), 650; 1
pl., dryuke, 275; *pret.* 3 *sing.*, drank,
965; dronk, 881; *subj. pr.* 3 *sing.*,
drynke, 1675; *imper. sing.*, þrynk
(*for* drynk), 995; *pp.*, dronken, 1576
drury, *a.*, dreary, 971, 1495
drynkon, *s.*, drink, 833
dryuest, *pr.* 3 *sing.*, drives, 206
dwelle, dwellon, *v.*, 220, 298, 303;
pr. 1 *sing.*, dwelle, 1493; *imper.
pl.*, dwelleþ, 341; *pr. pt.*, dwellyng,
325
dyademe, *s.*, diadem, 547
dygnyte, *s.*, dignity, 600
dynt, *s.*, blow, 666, 1248
dysoryue, *v.*, to describe, 1458

E

eche, *v.*, to increase, 1679
eft, *adv.*, afterwards, 597
eft-sones, *adv.*, at once, 1383, 1527
ek, *adv.*, also, 885
elde, *s.*, age, 93, 187
enchesoun, *s.*, occasion, 1027
encense, *s.*, incense, 123, 898
encreseþ, *pr.* 3 *sing.*, increases, 348
endyng, *s.*, ending, death, 728
enquere, *v.*, to inquire, 914
enqueste, *s.*, inquest, trial, 1411
ensample, *s.*, example, 202, 203
entendeth, *pr.* 3 *sing.*, attends, listens, 161
ententiuely, *adv.*, urgently, 73
enterly, *adv.*, entirely, 796
entier, *a.*, entire, 799
entre, *v.*, to enter, 1673; *subj. pr.* 3
sing., entre, 242

er, *adv.*, ere, 320, 1160
er, *conj.*, *see under* weþer *and* wher
ere, *s.*, ear, 241
erly, *see under* erthely
erthely, *a.*, earthly, 373, 851; erly
(*for* erthely), 1664
est, *s.*, east, 139
ete, *v.*, to eat, 268; *pr.* 2 *sing.*, etest,
773; *pret.* 2 *sing.*, ete, 2068; 3 *sing.*,
et, 1567; 3 *pl.*, eton, 260; ete,
263
euel, *s.*, evil, disease, 205, 1243
euere, *see under* yuer
eueryedel, *adv.*, every bit, 502
euon, *a.*, even, equal, 1895
excused, *pp.*, pardoned, 493
eyleþ, *pr.* 3 *sing.*, ails, 943; 3 *pl.*, eylen
(*for* sing ?), 1873
eyr, *s.*, air, 1088
eysel, cisel, *s.*, vinegar, 834, 965, 1345
eyȝe, *see under* ye

F

fade, *a.*, faded, colorless, 1182
fader, *s.*, father, 1, 347; *gen.* faderes,
276
fail(l)e, *v.*, to fail, to weaken, 346, 918;
pr. 3 *sing.*, failes, 884; faileþ, 955;
subj. pr. 1 *pl.*, faile, 803
falle, *v.*, to fall, 908, 1210; *pr.* 3 *sing.*,
falleth, 520, 930; 3 *pl.*, falle, 2116;
pret. 3 *sing.*, ful, 1465; *pp.*, falle,
1248, 1738; y-falle, 1241; fallon,
289
fals, *a.*, false, 478, 502, 1296; *pl.*,
false, 488
falwon, falwe, *v.*, to fade, to wither,
110, 645
fare, *pr.* 2 *pl.*, fare, act, 1732
faste, *adv.*, fast, firmly, 433, 979, 1556
fauchoun, *s.*, falchion, 1592
faynt, *a.*, faint, weak, 624; *comp.*,
faynter, 2197; *see* feynt
fede, feden, fedon, *v.*, to feed, 822, 832,
2214; *pr.* 3 *sing.*, fedeht, 45; fedeþ,
722; *pret.* 2 *sing.*, feddest, 207;
3 *sing.*, fedde, 38; *pp.*, fed, 264;
y-fed, 1641

feer, *a.*, fierce, 375
fel, *s.*, fell, skin, 2080
fol, *a.*, cruel, 400, 1195; *pl.*, felle, 1431; *comp.*, feller, 525
fel, *adv.*, very, 651
feld(e), *s.*, field, 94, 658
felde, *v.*, to fail of strength, 1555; *pr. pp.*, feldand, 1308; *see* folde
fele, felon, *v.*, to feel, 362, 586; *pr.* 3 *sing.*, feleþ, 321, 909; *pret.* 3 *sing.*, felte, 324, 1957
fele, *a.*, many, 467, 1941
fell, felle, *v.*, to fell, to overthrow, 1058, 1876; *pr.* 3 *sing.*, felleþ, 741; *pp.*, feld, 250, 673, 952; felt, 1960
feller, *a.*, *see under* fel
felly, *adv.*, cruelly, 244, 658
felonye, *s.*, wickedness, 1299
feloun, *s.*, felon, wretch, 222, 228
felawes, *s.*, fellows, companions, 1794
felawrede, *s.*, fellowship, 1796
fend, *s.*, fiend, 219, 225; *gen.*, fendes, 1650; *pl.*, fendes, 2180, 2186
fer, *adv.*, far, 43, 468, 1212; ferre, 140; fere, 441
fere, *s.*, company; in fere, together, 865
fers, *a.*, fierce, 27, 929, 1821
ferste, *a.*, first, 1261
ferþe, *a.*, fourth, 212
feste, *s.*, feast, 189, 257, 1611
feste, *v.*, to feast, 34
feteres, *s.*, fetters, 233
fette, *pret.* 3 *sing.*, took away, 725; *pp.*, fet, y-fet, fetched, 190, 1449
feynt, *a.*, faint, exhausted, 1555
fey3, *a.*, ? 188
fey3t, *s.*, faith, 2074
fille, fulle, *s.*, fill, 606, 995, 1524
fir, fyr, *s.*, fire, 198, 869; fier, 1546
flauour, *s.*, flavour, odour, 92
fle, flee, *v.*, to flee, 236, 330, 730, 1059; *pr.* 1 *sing.*, fle, 1505; 3 *sing.*, fleþ, 2025; *pret.* 3 *pl.*, fledde, 2180; *subj. pr.* 3 *pl.*, flen, 2186
flescly, *a.*, fleshly, 1301
flete, *v.*, to flow, 1178
fley, *pret.* 3 *sing.*, flew, 201, 709

florische, *v.*, to flourish, 974; *pr.* 3 *sing.*, florscheþ, 94
flour, *s.*, flower, 38, 94; *pl.*, floures, 97, 255
flourdelys, *s.*, 700
fode, *s.*, food, 1980
folde, *v.*, to fail, to wither, 645; *see* felde
folweþ, *pr.* 3 *sing.*, follows, 1506; *pret.* 3 *sing.*, folwed, 441
fo, foo, *s.*, foe, 201, 1059; *pl.*, fon, 503, 1704
fomen, *s.*, 1726, 2200
fordon, *v.*, to destroy, 945; *pr.* 3 *sing.*, fordoth, 858
for-feynt, *a.*, weak, exhausted, 2201
forgo, *v.*, 1849
forhed, *s.*, forehead, 573, 1190
forlet, *pret.* 3 *sing.*, abandoned, 1568
forloke, *pp.*, imprisoned, 1010
forlore, forlorn, *pp.*, lost, 130, 942, 1194, 1872
fors, *s.*, concern, heed, 1818
forsake, *v.*, 836, 851; *pr.* 2 *sing.*, forsakest, 1238; *pret.* 3 *sing.*, forsok, 167; forsoke, 444; *pp.*, forsake, 1284, 1725
forsoþe, *adv.*, *see under* soþe
forte, *for* for to, 799, 801, 967
forþfulle, *v.*, to fulfil, to accomplish, 1820; *imper. sing.*, forthfulle, 7; *pret.* 2 *sing.*, forthfuldest, 497; *pp.*, forthfuld, 819
forþer, *adv.*, further, 440
forþinketh, *pr.* 3 *sing.*, repents, 1129
for3eue, for3yue, *v.*, to forgive, 446, 2235; *pret.* 3 *sing.*, for3af, 448
fot, *s.*, foot, 930; *pl.*, fet, 365, 991, 1192
foule, *adv.*, foully, 1396
fouled, *pret.* 3 *sing.*, defiled, 1344
fram, *prep.*, from, 169, 208, 653, 816; from, 13
frankensent3, *s.*, frankincense, 132
fre, *a.*, free, gracious, 127, 287
frend, *s.*, friend, 400, 838; *pl.*, frendes, 314, 1268
fruyt, *s.*, fruit, 342, 724; frouyt, 1544

Glossary. 73

ful, *adv.*, fully, entirely, 16; very, 69, 169
fulfulle, *v.*, to fulfill, 1623; *pp.*, fulfilt, 867
fulle, *see under* fille
fully, *adv.*, 128
fulthe, *s.*, filth, 1305, 2025
fygth, fyȝt(h), *s.*, fight, 70, 1058, 1270
fynde, *v.*, 1291, 2009; *pr. 2 sing.*, fyndest, 829, 1999; *pret. 3 pl.*, fondón, 144; *pp.*, fonden(on), 100, 696; founde, 519; y-founde, 669, 1018
fyngres, *s.*, 414
fyȝt(e), fiȝte, *v.*, to fight, 658, 705, 729, 739; *pr. 2 sing.*, fyȝtest, 1596

G

game, *for* graue, 211
game, gamon, *s.*, game, amusement, 1276, 1394
gan, gonne, *see under* gynneþ
gentel, gentil, *a.*, 9, 1249
gere, *s.*, gear, 66
gerlond, *s.*, garland, 99
geten, *pp.*, got, 1052
ghyle, *see under* gyle
gildon, *a.*, golden, 1966
gilt, gylt, *s.*, guilt, 584, 1253, 1872
gilty, gylty, *a.*, guilty, 1084, 1226
gle, *s.*, glee, 1276
gloweþ, *pr. 3 sing.*, 869
gnawe, *pp.*, 214
go, gon, *v.*, 284, 295; *pr. 1 sing.*, 306; *2 sing.*, gost, 99; goth, *for 2nd per.*, 406; *3 sing.*, goth, 412, 500; *3 pl.*, gon, 1916; *pp.*, gon, 280, 596; y-gone, 97
god, *s.*, worldly good, 1334
god, *a.*, 191, 203; good, 1903; *pl.*, gode, 1809
godhede, *s.*, 657
godnesse, *s.*, goodness, 1663, 2053
gost, *s.*, spirit, 1237, 1622; Holy Ghost, 14, 1045
grame, *s.*, grief, 615, 1303
graue, *pp.*, engraved, 1835
graunte, *v.*, 2236; *pr. 2 sing.*, grantest, 811; *3 sing.*, grauteþ, 2170; *pret. 3 sing.*, graunted, 533; *imper. sing.*, graunte, 4
grene, *a.*, 1805, 1809, 2127
gret, *a.*, 150, 267; *pl.*, grete, 1339, 1846
grete, *v.*, to greet, 11, 1372; *pr. 1 sing.*, grete, 698; *pp.*, gret, 13
greue, *v.*, to grieve, 1816; *pr. 3 sing.*, greueþ, 471, 1608; *pret. 3 pl.*, greuede, 1941
grille, *a.*, harsh, 528
grisly, grysly, *a.*, horrible, 66, 1598
grone, *v.*, to groan, 642, 967; *pr. 3 sing.*, groneþ, 615, 1019
gronynge, *s.*, 1529
gropon, *v.*, to grope, 2062
grys, *s.*, a gray fur, 1614
gurd, *pp.*, girded about, 1321
gye, *v.*, to guide, 1222; *pret. 3 sing.*, gyed, 1783; *pp.*, gyed, 610
gyle, *s.*, guile, deceit, 1649, 2109; ghyle, 300
gyltles, *a.*, 406
gynneþ, *pr. 3 sing.*, begins, 518; *pret. 2 sing.*, gonne, 217; *3 sing.*, gan, 39, 151, 496; *3 pl.*, gonne, 230, 492, 1145; gonnen(on), 256, 285, 1432; gan, 992
gynnyng, *s.*, beginning, 2254

H

ha, han, *see under* haue
haberio(u)n, *s.*, small hauberk, 1591, 1603
haire, *s.*, hair-cloth, 1613; hayre, 1628
halsed, *pp.*, embraced, 30
halue, *s.*, half, part, 1877
halwen, *s.*, saints, 1779
ham, *see under* þei
hangeþ, *pr. 3 sing.*, 1784, 1792; *pret. 2 sing.*, hynge, 1217; *3 sing.*, hung, 638, 1517; heng, 1227; hyng, 1352; *imper. sing.*, hang, 1413; *pp.*, hanged, 781, 1478, 1564
happes, *s.*, lots, chances, 316
harde, *adv.*, firmly, unsparingly, 417, 426, 632, 750
harp(e), *s.*, 12, 1925

hastely, *adv.*, quickly, 1023
haue, hauen, han, *v.*, to have, 59, 137, 289, 772; ha, 288; *pr.* 1 *sing.*, haue, 267, 680; 2 *sing.*, hast, 8, 26; has þou, 767; hastou, 1157; 3 *sing.*, haþ, 20, 35; haht, 42; has, 102; haueþ, 539, 982; 1 *pl.*, han, 202; haue, 1000; 2 *pl.*, han, 1717; 3 *pl.*, han, 329, 455; hauon, 2249; *pret.* 2 *sing.*, haddest, 523, 1902; 3 *sing.*, hadde, 184, 261; 3 *pl.*, haddon, 880, 1446; *imper. sing.*, haue, 1326; *subj. pr.* 2 *sing.*, haue, 74; *negat.* nath, 584
hay, *s.*, 1002
hay, ? 1006
he, *pron.*, 31, etc.; *obj.*, him, 29, 152; hym, 30, 131; hyn, *for* hym, 594; *reflex.*, him, 557, 572
he, *pron.*, she, 1667; *see* sho *and Intro., p.*, xiv., *note* 3
he, *pron.*, they, 271; *see* þei
hed, *s.*, head, 574, 1368, 1450; heued, 540; hed ? 1973
hed, hede, *s.*, heed, 1033, 1737
held, *pret.* 3 *sing.*, 1007; *pp.*, holden, 248
hele, *s.*, health, well-being, 468, 678, 1086, 1091
hele, *v.*, to heal, 2018; *pr.* 2 *sing.*, helest, 205; 3 *sing.*, heleþ, 875
heled, *pret.* 3 *sing.*, hid, protected, 40
helle, *s.*, hill, 1843; *pl.*, helles, 1844
helle, *s.*, hell, 198, 240; *gen.*, helles, 2042
helle-put, *s.*, hell-pit, 1842, 1931
helle-pyne, *s.*, pain of hell, 780
helle-ȝates, *s.*, gates of hell, 1009
helm, *s.*, helmet, 572, 1601; *pl.*, helmes, 64
hem, *pron.*, *see under* þei
hende, *a.*, kindly, courteous, 1489
hennes, *adv.*, hence, 805
hent, y-hent, *pp.*, taken, 330, 554, 897, 1600
her, *s.*, hair, 1135, 1513, 1767
herde, *s.*, shepherd, 330
here, *v.*, to hear, 7, 913; *pr.* 1 *sing.*, here, 828, 1069; 2 *sing.*, herest, 833; 3 *pl.*, here, 1048, 1107; heron, 1112; *pret.* 1 *sing.*, herde, 1769; 3 *pl.*, herde, 2182
here, *poss. pron.*, their, 465; *see under* hure
herkon, *v.*, to harken, 170; *imper. sing.*, herkon, 847; herkene, 951, 2220
herte-blod, *s.*, heart's-blood, 693
herte-bok, *s.*, book of the heart, 1415
herte-rote, *s.*, root of the heart, 1062
hertly, *a.*, whole-hearted, 1708
hertly, *adv.*, heartily, 404
hestes, *s.*, hests, commands, 311
hete, *s.*, heat, 869, 1957, 2140
heþen, *adv.*, hence, 762
heued, *see under* hed
heuene, *s.*, heaven, 6, 13; heuon, 169; *gen.*, heuenes, 938
heyl, heil, *adj.*, 1, 592, 622
hid(d)on, *pret.* 3 *pl.*, hid, covered, 454, 1511; *pr. pt. used as s.*, hidynge, 1401; *pp.*, hud, 456, 1772; y-hud, 2164
hider, *adv.*, hither, 398, 1887
hidous, hydous, *a.*, hideous, 62, 511, 1417; hides, 450
hidynge, *see under* hiddon
hie, hy(e), *a.*, high, exalted, 46, 86, 895, 1103, 1217, 2091
hie, hye, *adv.*, high, 726, 1450
hit, hyt, *pron.*, it, 101, 102, 158
hiȝtest, *pr.* 2 *sing.*, promisest, 804
ho, *pron.*, who, 847, 1029
hok, *s.*, hook, 781
hol, *a.*, hale, whole, 814, 1016
holde, *a.*, faithful, 802
holly, *adv.*, wholly, 1214
homly, *adv.*, familiarly, in a homey way, 30
hond, *s.*, 23, 429; *pl.*, hondes, 1005, 1192; beron on honde, accused of, 503
hondes, *s.*, hounds, 1431
hongreþ, *pr.* 3 *sing.*, hungers, 517
hors, *s.*, horse, 1593; *pl.*, hors, 1587
hors, *a.*, hoarse, 160, 1836
hos, hose, *pron.*, whose, 92, 1034
hosebo(u)nde, *s.*, husband, 1682, 2007 *gen.*, hosebondes, 1660

Glossary. 75

hoso, woso, *pron.*, whoso, 147, 161, 756; hose, 311, 587
hundredfold, *used as adv.*, 1184
hure, *poss. pron., fem. sing.*, her, 87, 145; 3 *pl.*, their, 292, 355, 358; here, 465
hurte, *s.*, hurt, wound, 916

I

iche, *a.*, *see under* ilk
ilk, *a.*, each, 343; ilke, 308; iche, 451; euere ilk, every one, 55
ilke, *a.*, same, 221, 427, 1336
ille, *s.*, ill, wrong, 1441, 1733
invyroun, *s.*, environment, 1088
i-se, *v.*, to see, 309
iuge, *s.*, judge, 494, 501
iug(g)ement, *s.*, judgment, 1386, 1444, 1552
i-wete, *v.*, to understand, 589
iwys, ywys, *adv.*, certainly, 85, 472

K

kemon, *see under* com
kepe, *pr.* 1 *sing.*, keep, 1716; 3 *sing.*, kepeth, 311; *subj. pret.* 1 *sing.*, kepte, would be concerned about, 1526; *pp.*, y-kept, cared for, 1464
keste, *see under* kus
keuere, *v.*, to cover, 1761, 1870; *see* kouere
kne, *s.*, knee, 591, 1125; *pl.*, knes, 2116
knelon, *pr.* 3 *pl.*, kneel, 1048, 1125; *pret.* 3 *sing.*, kneledon, 1409
knetteþ, *pr.* 3 *sing.*, knits, 1992; *pp.*, knet, 1990
knotte, *s.*, 1991
knotty, *a.*, 1138, 1336, 1990
knowe, knawe, *v.*, 785, 1268; *pr.* 2 *sing.*, knowest, 1127; *pp.*, i-knowe, 757
knowyng, *s.*, knowing, knowledge, 1008
knyth, *s.*, knight, 1269, 1959
korendon, *see under* corone
kouere, *v.*, to cover, 1382; *see* keuere
kouþe, *adv.*, familiarly, 2163
kus, *v.*, to kiss, 1908; *pr.* 3 *sing.*,
kisseth, 391; *pret.* 3 *sing.*, keste, 153; *pp.*, y-kust, 1179
kussyng, *s.*, kissing, 1645
kyn, *s.*, 9, 1316
kyndam, *s.*, kingdom, 2250
kynde, *s.*, kind, nature, 19, 40, 2097
kyndely, *adv.*, according to kind or nature, 31
kyndest, *pret.* 2 *sing.*, *from* cennan, to beget? 1128

L

ladder, *s.*, 712; ledder, 713
lasse, *a.*, *comp.*, less, 316, 1333
lang, *a.*, long, 65
last(e), *v.*, 888, 980; *pr.* 3 *sing.*, lasteþ, 784, 1066; *subj. pr.* 3 *sing.*, last, 2063; *pr. pt.*, lastyng, reaching, 712
lastynge, *a.*, lasting, everlasting, 204
lauȝtre, *s.*, laughter, 1448
lawe, *s.*, 213, 809, 2097; *pl.*, lawes, 1793; *used of the period before Christ*, 27
lawe, *adv.*, low, 638, 786; *see* lowe
lay, *s.*, song, 1919
leche, *s.*, leech, physician, 292, 1874
lede, ledon, *v.*, to lead, 1098, 1211, 1658; *pret.* 3 *sing.*, ladde, 1981; *pp.*, lad, 204, 1496; led, 199, 499
lef, *s.*, leaf, 185, 226
lef, *a.*, lief, dear, 266, 1327; luf, 2048; *def.*, loue, 1225; *comp.*, leuere, 1676
leide, *see under* leyn
lem, *s.*, brightness, 1114
lene, *a.*, lean, 1839
lenest, *pr.* 2 *sing.*, give, bestow, 6; 3 *sing.*, leneþ, 465, 1387; *imper. sing.*, lene, 379; *pp.*, lent, 2157, 2221
lengur, *adv.*, longer, 220
lere, *s.*, face, cheek, 759, 1430, 1461
lered, MS. lereþ, *pp.*, learned, 692
lerned, *pret.* 3 *sing.*, learned, 445; *imper. sing.*, lerne, 861; *pl.*, lerneþ, 337
les, *v.*, to lose, 919; *pr.* 3 *sing.*, leseþ, 977, 2198; 3 *pl.*, luson, 1924; *pp.*, lorn, 564; y-lorn, 551, 1459
leste, *pret.* 3 *sing.*, pleased, 1580

Glossary.

lesteneþ, *imper. pl. for sing.*, 889
lete, *v.*, to let, allow, 530, 745; *pr.* 3 *sing.*, let, 522; *pret.* 3 *sing.*, let, 605; *imper. sing.*, lete, 280; let, 686; lat, 1625; *pp.*, let, 1010
lettres, *s.*, 589, 887, 1358; loue-lettre, 695
leue, *s.*, leave, departure, 284, 1283
leue, *a.*, *see under* lef
leue, leuon, *v.*, to believe, 356, 1815; *pr.* 1 *sing.*, leue, 2092
leue, *v.*, to leave, 438; *pr.* 3 *sing.*, leueþ, 162; *pp.*, left, 554
leue, *v.*, to live, 1288, 1293; *see* lyue
leuere, *a.*, *see under* lef
leyghe, *v.*, to laugh, 617; *pr. pt. used as s.*, leyȝhenge, 1401
leyn, *pr.* 3 *pl.*, lay, 631; *pret.* 3 *sing.*, leide, 1878; *pp.*, leid, 690, 1276; y-lied, 756; y-leyd, 1800; led, MS. ledon, laid on? 916
leyȝhenge, *see under* leyghe
lich, *a.*, like, 483, 754, 895, 2131; lych, 892, 2154; *see* lik
lif, lyf, *s.*, life, 114, 675; lyue, 1457, 2230; *gen.*, lyues, 1092; on lyue, alive, 530
lifte, *pret.* 3 *sing.*, lifted, 181
lighte, *pret.* 3 *sing.*, alighted, 169
lik, lyk, *a.*, like, 16, 84, 894; *see* lich
likneþ, *pr.* 3 *sing.*, compares, 113, 2138; likeneþ, is like, 2122; *pp.*, likned, 79, 82
likyng, *pr. pt. used as s.*, liking, enjoying, 1616
lilie-spryng, *s.*, spray of lilies, 939
lion, lioun, *s.*, lion, 517, 525; *gen.*, lyons, 1316
lion, *v.*, *see under* ly
lippes, *s.*, lips, 641, 1752, 1911
lisse, *s.*, comfort, relief, 321
listes, *s.*, lusts, 1300
litel, lytel, lytyl, *a.*, little, 299, 394, 1472
lith, *v.*, *see under* ly
liþ, *s.*, limb, 1762
lok(e), *v.*, to look, 616, 1131; *pr.* 1 *sing.*, loke, 421; *pret.* 2 *sing.*, lokedest, 1219; 3 *sing.*, lokede, 1174, 1177; *imper. pl.*, loketh, 317, 335
loke, *pp.*, locked, 829
long(e), *adv.*, long, for a long time, 770, 771, 2196
lore, *s.*, lore, teaching, 355, 679, 1995
lorere, *s.*, laurel, 556, 562, 986; lorer, 877
loude, *adv.*, loudly, 617
loue, louon, *v.*, to love, 77, 356, 667; *pr.* 3 *sing.*, loueþ, 312, 808; 2 *pl.*, loue, 305; *pret.* 2 *sing.*, louedest, 1159; 3 *sing.*, louede, 510; *subj. pr.* 3 *sing.;* loue, 308; *pret.* 3 *sing.*, louede, 569
louely, *adv.*, lovingly, 401
loue-lykyng, *s.*, joy of love, 685, 819
loues, *s.*, loaves, 207
loute, *v.*, to bend, bow down, 76
low, *a.*, lowly, humble, 1609
lowe, *adv.*, low, 169, 1267
luf, *a.*, *see under* lef
lulled, *pret.* 3 *sing.*, 156
luson, *see under* les
ly, lion, *v.*, to lie, 24, 1162; *pr.* 3 *sing.*, lith, 216, 1926; lyþ, 1267; liȝth, 1421; *pret.* 3 *sing.*, lay, 211, 1466
lych, *see under* lich
lycour, *s.*, liquor, 37, 994
lykyng, *s.*, liking, pleasure, 4, 364
lykyng, *a.*, pleasant, pleasing, 165, 1327, 1440
lylye-lyk, *a.*, like a lily, 639
lym, *s.*, limb, 1762
lyue, lyuon, *v.*, to live, 278, 2040, 2236; *subj. pret.* 2 *sing.*, liuedest, 859; *see* leue

M

mageste, *s.*, majesty, 896
maistrieþ, *pr.* 3 *sing.*, masters, 738
make, *s.*, mate, 1801
make, *v.*, 164, 165; *pr.* 1 *sing.*, make, 3, 307; 2 *sing.*, makest, 949, 1034; 3 *sing.*, maketh, 236, 572; 2 *pl.*, make, 1711; 3 *pl.*, maken, 476; *pret.* 2 *sing.*, madest, 257, 367; 3 *sing.*, made, 50, 282; maude, 262;

Glossary. 77

3 *pl.*, madon(en), 1148, 1476; *pr. pt.*, makyng, 1461; *pp.*, mad, 374, 376; made, 109; y-mad, 1320; maud, 1693, 1718, 1796

man, *s.*, 2, 112; *gen.*, mannes, 2, 213; *pl.*, men, 112; *gen. pl.*, mennes, 2030

manas, *s.*, menace, 1476

maner(e), *s.*, manner, custom, 56, 363, 555

mangerye, *s.*, feast, 262

marchaunt, *s.*, merchant, 393

mark, *s.*, target, 1711

marter, *s.*, martyr, 1955

mate, *a.*, weary, wretched, 1406

maud, *s.*, maid, 9, 16

may, *pr.* 1 *sing.*, 7, 83; 2 *sing.*, mayst, 1233; 3 *sing.*, may, 58, 346; 1 *pl.*, may, 59; 2 *pl.*, may, 52; *pret.* 1 *sing.*, mygthe, 127; 2 *sing.*, myʒtest, 399, 667; myʒt, 740, 836; 3 *sing.*, myght, 219; myʒte, 409, 636; 3 *pl.*, mygthe, 656; miʒton, 2156; *subj. pr.* 1 *sing.*, mowe, 1067; 3 *pl.*, mow, 344

maydonhoþ, *for* -hod ? *s.*, maidenhood, 1223

maymed, *a.*, maimed, 290

maystry(e), *s.*, mastery, 74, 261, 772

mede, *s.*, reward, 1160

medwe, *s.*, meadow, 1469; *pl.*, medwes, 2127

medled, *pp.*, mixed, 172, 834, 1866

mekely, *adv.*, 68; mekelyche, 1132

mervayle, *s.*, wonder, 917

mete, *s.*, meat, 35, 44, 1838

mete, *v.*, to meet, 256, 1830; *pp.*, met, 2208

meue, *v.*, to move, 56

meyne, *s.*, following, 332, 571

michel, *a.*; great, 968; *see* mikel

mikel, mykel, *a.*, much, great, 22, 41; mukel, 293, 1498, 2053; muchel, 2135

mirre, *s.*, myrrh, 132, 415

mo, *a.*, more, 233, 357, 1606

moder, moþer, *s.*, mother, 144, 148; *gen.*, moder, 948; moders, 1455

molde, *s.*, mold, earth, 1693

mole, *s.*, mark, blemish, 1672

mone, *s.*, moan, 277, 968; mon, 612

mone, *s.*, moon, 52, 907

morne, *v.*, to mourn, 1540; *pr.* 3 *sing.*, morneþ, 971, 1801; *pret.* 3 *pl.*, mornedon, 923; *pr. pt.*, mornyng, 1920

mornyng, *s.*, mourning, 277, 363, 1611

mornynge, *s.*, morning, 1279

most, *a.*, greatest, strongest, 558, 1046, 1119

mot, *pr.* 1 *sing.*, must, 438, 914, 1536; 2 *sing.*, most, 295, 2224; *subj. pr.* 2 *sing.*, mot., 1060; 3 *sing.*, mote, 4; mot, 1335

mowe, *s.*, heap, 113

mowe, *v.*, *see under* may

mowe, *pp.*, mowed, 1003

muchel, *a.*, *see under* mikel

muckel, *adv.*, greatly, 1679

mukel, *a.*, *see under* mikel

mulk, *s.*, *see under* mylk

murþe, *s.*, *see under* myrþe

myche, *a.*, much, great, 629; muche, 1453

mygtful, myʒtful, *a.*, mighty, 71, 1927

mykel, *adv.*, much, 1200

mylk, *s.*, milk, 32, 48; milk, 121; mulk, 42

mynstralcy, *s.*, 158

myrie, *a.*, merry, 972, 1773

myrþe, mirthe, *s.*, mirth, 384, 971; merthe, 938; murþe, 1071; *pl.*, myrthes, 164

mys, mysse, *v.*, to miss, to fail, 2036, 2112

myschief, *s.*, misfortune, 694; myschef, 1328

mysdo, mysdon, *pp.*, misdone, 582, 950, 1157

myʒt, myght, *s.*, might, power, 72, 249; *pl.*, myʒtes, 1119, 1621

N

naked, *a.*, 1386, 1387, 1530; nakud, 1517

namore, *adv.*, never more, 1280, 2050

natyuyte, *s.*, 1739

78 *Glossary.*

nede, *s.*, need, 387, 1159; *gen. used as adv.*, nedes, 1536
neider, *adv.*, neither, 1984; *see* neyþer
nekke, *s.*, neck, 117
nemne, *v.*, to name, 1037; *pp.*, nempned, 1099, 1121
ner, nere, *adv.*, near, 442, 628
neygheþ, *see under* nyʒhe
nobeleye, *s.*, nobility, 743
noght, no(u)ʒt, *s.*, naught, 160, 797, 1348
noied, *pret. 3 sing.*, annoyed, 19
note, *s.*, nut, 721
nought, no(u)ʒt, *adv.*, 19, 510, 849, 853, 955
ny, *adv.*, nigh, 387, 1218
nyghtyngale, nyʒtyngale, *s.*, 159, 1317
nyl, *v., see under* will
nyʒhe, *v.*, to approach, 1510; *pr. 3 sing.*, neygheþ, 390; *pret. 3 sing.*, neyghed, 442

O

o, *art.*, a, 914, 1038
oeuere, *s.*, attack? 666; (Cf. OF. oevre.)
of, *adv.*, off, 438, 1767
of, *prep.*, 1, 9; from, off, 537; by, 1472
offredon, *pret. 3 pl.*, offered, 131, 134
on, *art.*, an; 1184
on, *num.*, one, 1894, 2010, 2016; euere in on, forever, 1652, 2134
ones, *adv.*, once, 604, 1946
onlich, *adv.*, only, 197
onne, *adv.*, on, 998
opon, *a.*, open, 2061
opyn, *imper. sing.*, open, 2243
ordeyned, *pp.*, ordained, 896
ordre, *s.*, order, company, 1110, 1113; *pl.*, ordres, 1123
ost, *s.*, host, 1111, 1120
ouercome, *v.*, 409; *pr. 3 sing.*, ouercomeþ, 1938; *pret. 3 sing.*, ouercam, 984, 2109; *pp.*, ouercome, 228, 704; ouercomen(on), 982, 1588
ouergon, *pp.*, surpassed, 632
oureselue, *pron.*, 2195; oureself, 2199
outher, *conj.*, or, 175
out-spronge, *pp.*, sprung forth, 122
oyle, *s.*, oil, 1952

P

pal, *s.*, pall, a kind of cloth, 1614
paleis, *s.*, palace, 709
parceyved, *pret. 3 sing.*, perceived, 501
parten, *v.*, to part, depart, 279
party, *s.*, part, 1127
pase, *v.*, to depart, die, 1170; *see* passe
passe, *v.*, to pass, pass away, surpass, 1334; *pr. 3 sing.*, passeth, 258, 364; passet, 158; *3 pl.*, passen, 1724
pauyes, *s.*, pavis, a large shield, 63
pees, *s.*, peace, 68, 405
pellican, *s.*, 692
pelure, *s.*, a kind of fur, 1614
perce, *v.*, to pierce, 579, 1631; *pr. 3 sing.*, perseþ, 464; *pret. 3 sing.*, perced, 1022, 1023
pere, *s.*, peer, 8, 102
pereles, *a.*, 81
perre, *s.*, precious stones, jewelry, 551, 554
peynted, y-peynt, *pp.*, painted, 840, 1468, 1656
planetes, *s.*, 53
plates, *s.*, plates of armour, 64
plente, *s.*, 419, 821, 1615
pomegarnet, *s.*, pomegranate, 116
pore, *a.*, poor, 1312, 1332, 2028; *see* pouere
pottes, *s.*, pots, 190
pouere, *s., see under* powere
pouere, *a.*, poor, 1267
pouerte, *s.*, poverty, 1612, 1707
poudred, *pp.*, powdered, sprinkled, 700
powere, *s.*, 549; pouere, 698
poyn, MS. *reading for* poynt, *s.*, point, part, 1038
pray, *s.*, prey, 767, 770, 772; *see* preie
praye, *v.*, 386; *pr. 1 sing.*, pray(e), 353, 913, 2034; *1 pl.*, pray, 78; *pret. 3 sing.*, prayde, 2005; *imper. sing.*, praye, 2231; prey, 2237
prayse, prayson, preyson, *v.*, to praise, 8, 11, 128; *pr. 3 sing.*, preyseþ, 928; preiseþ, 932
praysyng, preysyng, *s.*, praising, 3, 2251; praiseworthiness, 864, 936
preie, *s.*, prey, 519, 1168; *see* pray

Glossary. 79

preisest, *pr.* 2 *sing.*, pressest, crushest, 845
presentȝ, *s.*, gifts, 131
preiere, preyer, *s.*, prayer, 367, 1637; prayere, 2170
premerole, pri(y)merole, *s.*, primrose, 96, 98, 2123; prumorole, 1671
pres, *s.*, press, retinue, 67
prest, *a.*, prompt, 1557
preue, *pr.* 1 *sing.*, prove, 44; 3 *sing.*, preueþ, 1964; *pret.* 3 *sing.*, proued, 1943
prikke, *s.*, prick, 586
pris, prys, *s.*, price, value, 81, 257
profre, *v.*, 2118
punches, *s.*, 1559
purgeth, MS. pugeþ, *pr.* 3 *sing.*, purges, prunes, 347
purpul, *s.*, 1614
put, *s.*, pit, 1255
putten, *pr.* 3 *pl.*, put, 1808; *pret.* 3 *sing.*, putte, 2094; 3 *pl.*, putten, 1577; *imper. sing.*, put, 734, 1622
pyght, *pp.*, fixed, 626, 630; pyȝt, 1572
pyne, *s.*, pain, 1189

Q

quake, *v.*, 225, 327; *pret.* 3 *sing.*, quok, 1502; 3 *pl.*, quaked, 2181
qued, *s.*, evil, sin, 473, 627, 778
quenchon, *v.*, 198; *pr.* 3 *sing.*, quencheth, 1379, 1546; *imper. sing.*, quench, 996; *pp.*, queynt, 2202
quest, *s.*, inquest, inquiry, 477; *see* enqueste
queynt, *see under* quenchon
quyte, *v.*, to acquit, free, 958; *pp.*, quyt, paid, requited, 1160; y-quyt, 2110

R

ras, *s.*, rush, attack, 1475, 1972
raue, *v.*, to rave, 671
receyueþ, *pr.* 3 *sing.*, receives, 2139
rede, *v.*, to read, 587, 1973; *pr.* 1 *sing.*, rede, 1064, 1533; *imper. sing.*, rede, 587
redeliche, *adv.*, readily, 1228

reherce, *pr.* 1 *sing.*, relate, 580
reisedest, *pret.* 2 *sing.*, raised, 208, 209
relese, *v.*, to release, 2172
reme, *s.*, realm, 970
renne, *v.*, to run, 1823, *pr.* 3 *sing.*, renneþ, 541; *pret.* 3 *sing.*, ran, 537, 775, 1342; 3 *pl.*, ronne, 635; ronnon, 1430, 1480; *pr. pt.*, rennyng, 1364
renton, *pret.* 3 *pl.*, rent, tore, 1513; *pp.*, rent, 768, 1142; y-rent, 620
reue, *v.*, to rob, 1520
reufely, *adv.*, ruefully, pitiably, 573
reuful, *a.*, 1257, 1350
reuly, *a.*, pitiable, 1182, 1416; rewly, 998; *see* ruly
reuthe, *s.*, ruth, pity, 763, 925; ruþe, 464
reward, *s.*, regard, comparison, 2128, 2191
rewe, *v.*, to pity, 1880
rewly, *see under* reuly
reyn, *s.*, rain, 908
richesse, *s.*, riches, 395; ryches, 1612
right, riȝt, *adv.*, very, 296; just, 297, 438, 612
riȝtful, *a.*, righteous, 514
riȝtfulnes, ryȝtfulnesse, *s.*, righteousness, 86, 146
roche, *s.*, rock, 1981
rode, *s.*, rood, 532, 915
rode-tre, *s.*, rood-tree, 512, 1336
rody, *a.*, ruddy, 115; *comp.*, rodier, 2124
rof, *s.*, roof, 1656
rogged, *see under* rugged
romaunce, *s.*, 1697
rore, *v.*, to roar, 518
roser, *s.*, rose-bush, 105, 702
rote, *s.*, root, 1631
rowe, *s.*, row; on rowe, in turn, 270
rud, *s.*, reed, 969
rugged, *a.*, rough, blunt, 1139; rogged 1362
ruly, *a.*, pitiable, 463, 538; *see* reuly
rype, *v.*, to ripen, 185
rys, *s.*, branch, twig, 2124
ryse, *v.*, to rise, 2037; *pret.* 3 *pl.*, ryson, 1146; *pp.*, rise, 2066
ryȝtwisnesse, *s.*, righteousness, 2091

Glossary.

S

saffere, saphir, s., sapphire, 550, 2149
salue, s., salve, 1878
saue, *prep.*, except, 1149
saule, soule, s., soul, 220, 1547; *pl.*, soules, 234, 2115
sauon, v., to save, 1506; *pr.* 2 *sing.*, sauest, 716
sauyour, s., savior, 390, 421
sautrye, s., psaltery, 1274
sawes, s., sayings, 1735
schewed, *see under* shewe
scories, s., scourges, 634, 1553, 1750
se, see, s., see, seat, 895, 1052, 1106, 2227
se, see, s., sea, 51, 1244
se, sen, v., to see, 22, 52, 148, 274; *pr.* 1 *sing.*, se, 424, 425; 3 *sing.*, seþ, 1661; *pret.* 2 *sing.*, syc, 918; 3 *sing.*, sy, 179, 1153; sey, 711; say, 703, 1460; saw, 1181; 3 *pl.*, sion, 1452; *subj. pr.* 3 *sing.*, se, 1031; *imper. sing.*, se, 1915; *pp.*, sene, 15, 311; seyn, 184
seek, *see under* souke
sekenes, *see under* siknesse
sekeþ, *pr.* 3 *sing.*, 1670; *pp.*, souȝt, 770
selde, a., rare, 188
seler, s., cellar, 1673
seluer, s., silver, 35
sely, a., humble, simple, 1597
semblant, s., countenance, 457, 483, 2023
sem(e)ly, a., seemly, 872, 911
semely, *adv.*, seemly, fittingly, 115
senatour, s., senator, 1855; *pl.*, senatoures, 878
sende, v., 1630; *pret.* 2 *sing.*, sendest, 2071; 3 *sing.*, sente, 1405, 1771; *subj. pr.* 2 *sing.*, sende, 826; *imper. sing.*, send(e), 361, 816; sent, 733; *pp.*, sent, 1443; send, 1887
septre, s., scepter, 599, 607
sereþ, *pr.* 3 *sing.*, grows sere, 1806
serful, a., sorrowful, 1309
seruage, s., servitude, 958, 1012
seruant, s., servant, 793; seuant, MS., 1369; *pl.*, seruantȝ, 313, 350

serwe, s., sorrow, 178, 615; sorwe, 327, 334; serewe, 320; *pl.*, serwes, 2246
sesse, *pr.* 3 *pl.*, cease, 1066
se-sterre, s., sea-star, applied to Jesus, 1098
sete, s., seat, 2076
sette, *pr.* 1 *sing.*, set, 1040, 1348; *pret.* 2 *sing.*, settest, 797; 3 *sing.*, sette, 53, 726; 3 *pl.*, setton, 591; *imper. sing.*, set, 1324, 2188; *pp.*, set, 29, 887; y-set, 417, 540; seet, 115
seyn, v., to say, 1807; *pr.* 1 *sing.*, sey, 300; say, 1899; 3 *sing.*, seþ, 782; seyth, 1134, 1897; *pret.* 2 *sing.*, seydest, 265; seidest, 295; seides, 397; 3 *sing.*, said, *for* saiþ? 122; seide, seyde, 224, 243, 1049; 3 *pl.*, seidon, 592; *subj. pret.* 1 *sing.*, saide, 126; *imper. sing.*, sey, 237; *pp.*, said, 498, 1736
shad, *pp.*, shed, 1452
shal, *pr.* 1 *sing.*, 11, 301; 2 *sing.*, shalt, 279; 3 *sing.*, shal, 130, 315; 2 *pl.*, shal, 273; shul, 303, 328; shulle, 326, 327; 3 *pl.*, shul, 330; shulle, 1654; shullon(en), 309, 352, 355; *pret.* 1 *sing.*, sholde, 1164; 2 *sing.*, sholdest, 860, 1458; 3 *sing.*, sholde, 331, 562; shulde, 2064, 2086; 1 *pl.*, sholde, 278; sholden, 805; 2 *pl.*, sholde, 611; 3 *pl.*, sholden(on), 289, 888
shapest, *pr.* 3 *sing.*, makest ready, 873; *pret.* 3 *sing.*, shop, 244; *pp.*, shape, 1586
sheld, s., shield, 246, 657; *pl.*, sheldes, 63
shende, v., to destroy, bring to grief, 855; *pr.* 3 *sing.*, shent, 481; *pp.*, shent, 371, 619; y-shent, 1243, 2222
shendshyp, s., dishonour, disgrace, 471
shewe, v., to show, 799; *pr.* 3 *sing.*, sheweth, 1963; *pret.* 2 *sing.*, shewedest, 2051, 2060; 3 *pl.*, shewdon, 1477; *pp.*, schewed, 139
shipman, s., sailor, 1962; *gen.*, shipmannes, 1097; *pl.*, shipmen, 282

Glossary. 81

sho, *pron.*, she, 82, 84, etc.; *obj.*, hure, 1219, 1220; *see* he
shonde, *s.*, dishonour, shame, 597, 624, 717
shote, *pr.* 2 *pl.*, shoot, 1712
shouon, *pret.* 3 *pl.*, shoved, 1558
shour, *s.*, assault, 416
shut, *pp.*, fastened, 1841
shynest, *pr.* 2 *sing.*, shinest, 5; 3 *sing.*, shyneth, 80, 391; 3 *pl.*, shynon, 871; *pr. pt.*, shynyng, 1996
signe, *s.*, sign, token, 1404; syne, 2051
sike, *a.*, *see under* syk
siker, *a.*, secure, 1054
siknesse, syknesse, *s.*, sickness, 292, 2211; sekenes, 1085
sipresse, *s.*, cypress, 1654
singe, synge, *v.*, 1280, 1919; *pr.* 3 *sing.*, syngeþ, 1665; *pret.* 3 *sing.*, sang, 159; song, 171; *subj. pret.* 1 *sing.*, songe, 126; *pr. pt.*, syngyng, 1667
sit, *pr.* 3 *sing.*, 548, 2227; 3 *pl.*, sitton, 407; *pret.* 3 *pl.*, seton, 1515
sithe, *conj.*, since, 401
siþes, *s.*, sides, 1823
siþþe, *conj.*, since, 668, 817; sithen, 815
siþen, *adv.*, then, in addition, 1999
skyl(e), *s.*, reason, 581, 790; skele, 1849; *pl.*, skiles, 2082
slake, *v.*, to slake, slacken, 163, 176, 1072
sle, *v.*, to slay, 750, 1481; *pr.* 2 *sing.*, slest, 1474, 2107; 3 *sing.*, sleþ, 676, 742, 1369; *imper. sing.*, sle, 1295, 1297; *pp.*, slayn, 137, 280, 673; y-slawe, 252, 810
smarte, *a.*, sharp, stinging, 640
smerte, *pret.* 3 *sing.*, pained, 1024; *pp.*, smerte, 463
smyteþ, *pr.* 3 *sing.*, *for* 2 *sing.* ?, 931; *pret.* 2 *sing.*, smyte, 358; 3 *pl.*, smeten, 601; *pp.*, smyte, 428, 462, 902; smyton, 459, 751
sobrenesse, *s.*, sobriety, 1313
soden, *pp.*, boiled, 1952
sodeyn, *a.*, sudden, 2072
softe, *adv.*, softly, low, 495
solas, *s.*, solace, 382, 1053, 1284; *dat.*, solace, 302

somdel, *adv.*, somewhat, 2246
sone, *s.*, son, 1, 937; *gen.* sones, 1174
sone, *adv.*, straightway, 240, 296, 860
sonne, sunne, *s.*, sun, 51, 900, 1013
sonne-bem, *s.*, sunbeam, 910
sonne-lyȝt, *s.*, sunlight, 903
sor, *s.*, sore, disease, 408
sore, *adv.*, sorely, 315, 359
sort, *s.*, lot, chance, 383
sortayn, *s.*, certainty, 1892
sory, *a.*, sorrowful, painful, 586, 972, 1165, 2215
sotil, *a.*, cunning, skilful, 10
soþe, *s.*, truth, 901; for soþe, 289, 737
souke, *v.*, to suck, 2239; *pr.* 3 *sing.*, souketh, 32, 124, 1671; 3 *pl.*, soukon, 1436; *pret.* 3 *sing.*, seek, 48; sok, 1188
soun, *s.*, sound, 227, 1055
soune, *subj. pr.* 3 *sing.*, sound, 12
sparres, *s.*, spars, beams, 1653
sparwe, *s.*, sparrow, 709
spatton, *pret.* 2 *pl.*, spat, 1720; 3 *pl.*, spatton, 452, 2006
speke, *v.*, 437, 440; *pr.* 1 *sing.*, speke, 1535; 2 *sing.*, spekest, 401; 3 *sing.*, speketh, 111, 627; *pret.* 2 *sing.*, spak(e), 272, 495, 505; speke, 2069; *subj. pr.* 1 *sing.*, speke, 125, 1213; *pret.* 3 *sing.*, spake, 1426
spende, *v.*, to spend, expend, 693; *pp.*, y-spent, 1244
spere, *s.*, sphere, 55
spille, spylle, spillon, *v.*, to spill, destroy, 58, 60, 526; *pr.* 1 *sing.*, spille, 1285; *pret.* 3 *sing.*, spilte, 136; 3 *pl.*, spilton, 514; *pp.*, spilt, 1236; y-spylt, 1254
spores, *s.*, spurs, 1594
spotel, *s.*, spittal, 840, 1180, 1344
sprede, *v.*, to spread, 39, 992; *pp.*, sprad, 1780
spryng, *s.*, spray, twig, 2130
sprynge, *v.*, to spring, to dawn, to flourish, 491, 1004; *pr.* 3 *sing.*, springeþ, 106, 994; *pret.* 2 *sing.*, sprang, 98; 3 *sing.*, sprang, 103, 369; *imper. pl.*, spring, 343
stan-naked, *a.*, stone-naked, 1762

Glossary.

stedes, *s.*, steeds, 61, 1587
sterep, *pr.* 3 *sing.*, steers, 85
sterne, *a.*, stern, unyielding, 75, 416, 2167
sterre, *s.*, star, 5, 139; *pl.*, sterres, 52, 907
sterte, *pret.* 3 *sing.*, started, 1484, 1541
steuene, *s.*, saying, words, 89, 2000; voice, 2069
stike, *v.*, to stick, to be fastened, 1854; *pret.* 3 *sing.*, stak, 979
stille, *adv.*, still, quietly. 500, 505, 1479
stilled, *pret.* 3 *sing.*, 152
stonde, stonden, *v.*, to stand, 504, 1218; *pr.* 1 *sing.*, stonde, 1713; 3 *sing.*, stant, 1380, 1386; stand, 1762; *pret.* 2 *sing.*, stode, 505; 3 *sing*, stod, 524, 1419; *imper. sing.*, stond, 830; *pr. pt.*, standyng, 1760
stounde, *s.*, time, 427, 951
stour, *s.*, conflict, 742, 984, 2175
stoute, *a.*, proud, stubborn, strong, 75, 886, 1363
strengest, *a.*, strongest, 827
stringes, *s.*, 163
stude, *s.*, stead, place, 1601
stydefast, *a.*, steadfast, 317
stye, *v.*, to mount, 1929; *pret.* 2 *sing.*, sty, 2070; 3 *sing.*, stey, 710
styf, *a.*, stiff, firm, 75, 962
stynkynd, *a.*, stinking, 1308
stynton, *pret.* 3 *pl.*, stopped, 1365
suffraunce, *s.*, endurance, patience, 1708
suffre, *v.*, to suffer, to permit, 737, 744; *pr.* 1 *sing.*, suffre, 1608; 2 *sing.*, suffrest, 2020; 3 *sing.*, suffrep, 957; suffred *for-*þ, *319, 416; *pret.* 2 *sing.*, suffredest, 490, 800; soffredyst, 795; 3 *sing.*, suffrede, 1132, 1211; suffred, 1420; *imper. pl.*, suffrep, 299
summe, *pron.*, some, 206; *see* som
sumtyme, *adv.*, once, at one time, 555, 1187
suþþe, *s.*, sight, 1942
swattest, *pret.*, 2 *sing.*, sweated, 368; *sing.*, swette, 644

swete, *adv.*, sweetly, 12
sweteliche, *adv.*, sweetly, 1377
sweuene, *s.*, dream, vision, 711
swich, *a.*, such, 855, 2010
swonken, *pp.*, toiled, 1575
swoun, *s.*, swoon, 1466
swoune, *v.*, to swoon, 578
swyde, *adv.*, very, 315, 495; swythe, 1155
swythe, *adv.*, quickly, 306; *see* swyde
sy, *see under* se, *v.*
syk, *a.*, sick, 1015; *pl.*, sike, 1016
syke, *v.*, to sigh, 359; *pr.* 3 *sing.*, sykeþ, 1015; *pret.* 3 *sing.*, siked, 602
sykeþ, *pr.* 3 *sing.*, sinks, 1242
sykernesse, *s.*, surety, 2054
sykynge, *s.*, sighing, 1529
syne, *s.*, sign, 2051; *see* signe
synne, *s.*, sin, 196, 1003; *pl.*, synnes, 2083
sytole, *s.*, citole, 1275
syþe, *s.*, scythe, 1003

T

tak, take, *v.*, to take, to understand, to give to, 112, 175, 1033; *pr.* 2 *sing.*, takest, 948, 1237; 3 *sing.*, takeþ, 1490; taket, 787; 3 *pl.*, taken, 1727; *pret.* 2 *sing.*, toke, 269, 1220; 3 *sing.*, tok, 47, 104; 3 *pl.*, toke, 284, 1428; tokon, 598, 1704; *imper. sing.*, tak, 812; *pp.*, take, 1266, 1726; taken, 88; y-take, 328, 764
talent, *s.*, wish, 906
targe, *s.*, a small shield, 63
tasse, *s.*, heap, rabble, 1598
teche, *v.*, to teach, 1680, 1758; *pret.* 2 *sing.*, tauȝtest, 385; 3 *sing.*, tauȝte, 675, 2073; *pp.*, tauȝt, 1045
telle, tellon, *v.*, 83, 864, 1438; *pr.* 1 *sing.*, telle, 297, 849; 3 *pl.*, tellon, 2001; *pret.* 3 *pl.*, toldon, 1739; *imper. sing.*, tel, 249
tene, *s.*, injury, 1272
tene, *v.*, to harass, 315
tete, *s.*, teat, 31, 36, 1188
tho, *conj.*, when, 184

Glossary. 83

thorw, *prep.*, through, 28, 72 ; thurw, 445
thousindes, *num.*, thousands, 207
thref, *pret.* 3 *sing.*, throve, 186
til, tyl, *prep.*, to, 87, 712, 1476, 2212
to, *num.*, two, 154, 1005, 1223, 1911
to-broke, *pp.*, shattered, 2190
to-breste, *v.*, to burst completely, 567
to-drawe, *pp.*, torn out, 1135, 1142
to-flawe, *pp.*, flayed, 1136
to-fore, *prep.*, before, 492, 494
to-forn, *adv.*, before, 319
to-gydere, *adv.*, together, 1278 ; to-gyderes, 275
tokenyng(e), *s.*, token, tokening, 133, 713 ; toknyng, 507
tonge, *s.*, tongue, 121, 627 ; tonke, 10
topace, *s.*, topaz, 2150
to-rend, *pr.* 3 *pl.*, rend, tear to pieces, 1436 ; *pp.*, to-rent, 735, 1137
tornen, *see under* turne
tornement, turnement, *s.*, 661, 1551
tour, *s.*, tower, 1054
traille, *s.*, branch, offshoot, 345, 1249
trauaile, *s.*, travail, 18 ; trauyle, 644
trauayleþ, *pr.* 2 *pl.*, toil, 335
traytour, *see* tretour
tre, *s.*, tree, the cross, 1138, 1152 ; *pl.*, trees, 1846
trespas, *s.*, 445, 447, 2234
treto(u)r, traytour, *s.*, traitor, 389, 1372, 1373
trey, *s.*, affliction, 1272
trist, *s.*, trust, 1230
trompe, *s.*, trumpet, 223, 1055 ; *pl.*, trompes, 62, 1589
trone, *s.*, throne, 652
trowe, *pr.* 1 *sing.*, believe, 749, 837
trynyte, *s.*, 133
turne, tornen, *v.*, to turn, 1696, 2086, 2106 ; *pr.* 3 *sing.*, turneþ, 905, 975 ; torneþ, 1302 ; 1 *pl.*, tornon, 2205 ; *pret.* 3 *sing.*, turned, 1582, 2096 ; tornde, 191 ; *pp.*, tornd, 322, 614
turnement, *see* tornement
turtil, *s.*, turtle-dove, 1315 ; turtel, 1801 ; *see* turtur
turtur, *s.*, turtle-dove, 708

þ

þan, þanne, *adv.*, then, 162, 201, 219 ; þon, 284
þey, *pron.*, *see under* þei
þef, *s.*, thief, 252, 406, 1227 ; *pl.*, defes, 1792
þei, *conj.*, though, 893, 934
þoi, þey, *pron.*, they, 75, 134 ; he *once*, 271 ; þay *once*, 594 ; *obj.*, hem, 76, 141, 247 ; ham *once.* 2157 *reflex.*, hem, 591
þenke, þenkon, *v.*, to think, 150, 285, 570 ; *pr.* 1 *sing.*, þenke, 1240, 1537 ; 3 *sing.*, þenkeþ, 323 ; *pret.* 1 *sing.*, þoȝte, 1163 ; 3 *sing.*, þoȝte, 1978
þet, *pron.*, that? or perhaps a miswriting for deþ? 371
þiselue, *see under* þou
þrikke, *s.*, thrust, 585
þinketh, *pr.* 3 *sing. imperson.*, seems, 559, 669 ; þenketh, 831
þo, *art.*, the, 602, 636, 792, 887
þo, *pron.*, those, 263, 283, 865
þo, tho, *adv.*, then, 365, 508, 618 ; þoo, 642
þorlest, *pr.* 2 *sing.*, pierce, 1521, 1594
þou, *conj.*, though, 2095
þrawe, *see under* þrowe
þrowe, *s.*, space of time, 170, 269 ; þrawe, 637
þrostel, *s.*, throstle, 1318
þruste, *pret.* 3 *pl.*, thrust, 1579 ; *pp.*, þrist, 1782
þrynk, *see under* drinke
þurst, *s.*, thirst, 996
þuse, *a.*, those, 357, 1123, 1323

V

vanyschon, *pr.* 1 *pl.*, vanish, 2203
vche, *pron.*, each, 2117
venym, *s.*, venom, 392, 1868
veray, verray, *a.*, true, 339, 711 ; verrey, 857
verrayliche, *adv.*, verily, 425
vertue, *s.*, 551
veyne, *s.*, vein, channel, 647

vilenye, *s.*, villainy, 459 ; vylonye, 1397
viole, *s.*, stain, spot, 95
vnder-fonge, *v.*, to seize, 769
vnicorn, *s.*, applied to Christ, 26, 1851
vnkynde, *a.*, unkind, unnatural, 807, 1499
vnryʒt, *s.*, unright, 453
vnsauory, *a.*, tasteless, 1304
vnwys, *a.*, 393, 831.

W

wake, *v.*, to wake, stir, 1633 ; *pr.* 3 *sing.*, waketh, 485 ; 3 *pl.*, wake, 226, 1914
wal, *s.*, whale, 1731
wan, wanne, *adv.*, when, 820, 1758
war, *conj.*, whether, 1749
ware, *s.*, 215, 2205
waschest, *pr.* 2 *sing.*, wash, 194 ; waschest, 843 ; 3 *sing.*, wascheþ, 1252 ; *pret.* 3 *sing.*, wisch, 365 ; wesch, 1879
wath, *a.*, what, 800, 868
wederes, *s.*, storms, 57
wele, *s.*, weal, 20, 677, 1538
welkeþ, *pr.* 3 *sing.*, withers, fades, 849, 853, 973, 1859 ; 1 *pl.*, welke, 2204 ; *pp.*, welked, 93, 97, 974
welkene, *s.*, welkin, 1468
welle, *s.*, well, spring, 197, 369 ; *pl.*, welles, 993
welle-spryng, *s.*, well-spring, source, 650, 686
wem, *s.*, spot, 1672, 2084
wende, *v.*, to go, depart, 805, 1490, 2090 ; *pr.* 1 *pl.*, wendon, 2206 ; *pret.* 3 *sing.*, wente, 141 ; went, 960 ; *subj. pr.* 2 *sing.*, wende, 1325 ; *pp.*, went, 1538, 2158
wendyng(e), *s.*, departing, 268, 1920
wene, *pr.* 1 *sing.*, suppose, judge, 985, 1810 ; 2 *sing.*, wenest, 672 ; *subj. pr.* 2 *sing.*, wene, 674
wepe, *v.*, to weep, 151, 155, 423 ; *pr.* 1 *sing.*, wepe, 1715 ; 3 *sing.*, wepeþ, 1666 ; *pret.* 3 *sing.*, wep, 959, 1027 ;

wepte, 1155 ; *subj. pr.* 1 *sing.*, wepe, 432 ; *pr. pt.*, wepynge, 256 ; *used as a.*, 1309
were, *s.*, doubt, 1172
werk, *s.*, work, miracle, 455, 1964 ; *pl.*, werkes, 188, 1809
wermes, wormes, *s.*, 2213, 2218 ; wormys, 214 ; *gen.*, wormes, 215 ; wermes, 2090
wermot, *s.*, wormwood, 481, 832, 1861
werne, *v.*, to refuse, 2168, 2242
werres, *s.*, wars, 701
werse, *a. and adv.*, worse, 1212, 1810
weþer, *conj.*, whether, 675, 678 ; er, for weþer ? 677
weykeþ, *pr.* 3 *sing.*, falls, droops, 762
weyle, *v.*, to wail, 360 ; *pr.* 1 *sing.*, weile, 427
wex(e), *v.*, to wax, 39, 920 ; *pr.* 3 *sing.*, wexeth, 468, 474 ; waxeth, 999 ; 3 *pl.*, wexon, 2152 ; *pret.* 3 *sing.*, wax, 538, 921 ; wex, 640, 641 ; *subj. pr.* 3 *sing.*, wexe, 436 ; *pr. pt.*, wexinge, 2104 ; *pp.*, woxen(on), 187, 484, 1011 ; woxe, 1813
whar-to, *adv.*, to what purpose, 1689
what, *used in exclamation*, 1185
wheles, *s.*, wheels, 1976
wher, *adv.*, whether, 1755 ; er, *conj.*, for wher ? 677 ; *see* weþer
whete, *s.*, wheat, 1837
while, *s., see under* wyle
while, *s.*, while, space of time, 295, 299 ; *gen. used as conj.*, 416, 1691
whiles, *see under* while
wich, *pron.*, which, 111, 1902, 2112
wikked, wykked, *a.*, wicked, 510, 1149, 1195 ; *pl.*, wikkede, 1566
wil, *v., see under* wole
wipte, *pret.* 3 *sing.*, wiped, 1777
wirketh, *see under* worchest
wis, *v.*, to show, make known, 960
wise, wyse, *s.*, way, manner, 2038, 2117
wite, wyte, *v.*, to know, 868, 901, 1189 ; *pr.* 1 *sing.*, wot, 1231, 1494 ; 3 *sing.*, wot, 333, 1074, 1738 ; 2 *pl.*, wite, 413 ; *negat. pr.* 1 *sing.*, not, 1815

Glossary.

withstonde, wyþstonde, *v.*, to resist, 70, 718; *pret.* 2 *sing.*, wiþstode, 201

witnesse, *s.*, witness, testimony, 478, 1997; witnes, 1953

witnessen, *pr.* 3 *pl.*, witness, 1970; *pret.* 3 *sing.*, witnesset, 1939

witty, *a.*, intelligent, 1709

wiþdrow, *pret.* 3 *sing.*, withdrew, 1143

wo, *a.*, woful, sad, 1185, 1426

wod, *a.*, mad, enraged, 135; *def.*, wode, 485; *pl.*, wode, 1139, 1435

wo-bygon, *a.*, woe-begone, 949, 1366

wois, woys, *s.*, voice, 160, 225

wole, *pr.* 1 *sing.*, will, wish, 350; wil, 313; 2 *sing.*, wolt, 820, 901, 2174; wilt, 579, 739; wylt, 1043; 3 *sing.*, wol(e), 1168, 1208, 1414, 2172; wele, 1098; wyl, 789, *pret.* 1 *sing.*, wolde, 437, 851; 2 *sing.*, woldest, 530, 2032; 3 *sing.*, wolde, 120, 137; 3 *pl.*, wolde, 288; woldon, 1418; *subj. pr.* 3 *sing.*, wole, 2246; *pret.* 3 *sing.*, wolde, 1161; *negat.*, nyl, 1210

wolf, *s.*, 482, 1600; *gen.*, wolues, 1315; *pl.*, wolues, 1142, 1435

wonder, *a.*, wonderful, 21, 33, 787

worchest, *pr.* 2 sing., work, 835; 3 *sing.*, worcheth, 57; wercheth, 334; wirketh, 789; *pret.* 3 *sing.*, wrouȝte, 188; wroȝte, 981, 1566; wroghte, 272; 3 *pl.*, wroghton, 234; *pp.*, wroȝt, 455, 1424

wordly, *a.*, worldly, 1078

wordy, *a.*, *see under* worþi

wordynesse, *s.*, worthiness, 2136

world, wordle, *s.*, world, 93, 315, 331; worle, MS. *reading*, 1696; *gen.*, wordles, 364, 1649; wordes, 1988

wormete, *a.*, worm-eaten, 2093

worþ, *subj. pr.* 3 *sing.*, be, 1473

worþi, worþy, *a.*, worthy, 985, 1166, 1488; wordy, 809

woso, *pron.*, whoso, 161; *see* hoso

wrake, *s.*, vengeance, 835; *see* wreche

wrangful, *a.*, unjust, 477

wrecches, *s.*, wretches, 1139

wreche, *s.*, vengeance, 1207, 1262

wrenches, *s.*, tricks, deceptions, 1650

writ, *s.*, Holy Writ, 111, 122

writon, *v.*, to write, 884; *pr.* 2 *sing.*, writest, 842; *pret.* 3 *sing.*, wrot, 883; *subj. pr.* 1 *sing.*, wryte, 1213; 2 *sing.*, write, 1457; *imper. sing.*, write, 695; writ, 1350; wryȝt, 1061; *pp.*, writon, 329, 886; i-write, 590; wryte, 1190

wroke, y-wroke, *pp.*, avenged, 656, 1256

wyde, *adv.*, widely, 1021

wyle, *s.*, cunning, wile, 1650; while, 2110

wyf, *s.*, wife, 1678; *gen.*, wyfes, 1862

wynde, *pr.* 2 *pl.*, wind, twist, 414; *pp.*, y-wounde, 412

wynne, *v.*, to win, 796; *pret.* 3 *sing.*, wan, 245; *pp.*, y-wonne, 964, 2141

wyt, *s.*, wit, intelligence, 112

Y

y-drust, *pp.*, covered, 1180

ye, *s.*, eye, 625, 1398, 1930; þe, MS. *reading*, 1834; eyȝe, 999; *pl.*, yon, 1745

y-fet, *see under* fette

y-lauȝt, *pp.*, caught, rescued, 882

y-lied, y-leyd, *see under* leyn

y-nome, *pp.*, taken, 410

yon, *s.*, *see under* ye

yron, *s.*, iron, 869, 1424, 1519

y-spreynt, *pp.*, sprinkled, 1467

y-strept, *pp.*, stripped, 1463

yuer, *s.*, ivory, 1655, 1835; euere, 839

ȝ

ȝates, *s.*, gates, 1842

ȝe, *adv.*, yea, 679

ȝe, *pron.*, ye, 52, 273; *obj.*, ȝow, ȝou, you, 268, 298, 1714

ȝelle, *v.*, to yell, 1432

ȝelt, *pr.* 3 *sing.*, yields, 1798

ȝerned, *pp.*, yearned for, 680

ȝesterday, *adv.*, yesterday, 1757, *etc.*

ȝet, *adv.*, yet, 231, 861; ȝit, 889, 913 ȝut, 1787

ȝif, *conj.*, if, 120, 751, 807; ȝyf, 1580
ȝifte, *s.*, gift, 182; *pl.*, ȝiftes, 134
ȝiue, ȝiuon, ȝyuon, *v.*, to give, 556, 959, 966, 1164; *pr.* 2 *sing.*, ȝeuest, 834; 3 *sing.*, ȝeueth, 856, 1381; ȝiueþ, 1008; *pret.* 2 *sing.*, ȝeue, 196; ȝef, 259; 3 *sing.*, ȝaf, 713, 970, 1519; *imper. sing.*, ȝif, 434; *pp.*, ȝiuon, 689; ȝiue, 1447; ȝoue, 969

ȝong, *a.*, young, 1464; *def.*, ȝonge, 155

ȝore, *adv.*, long, for a long time, 680

ȝoure, *poss. pron.*, your, 317, 336

ȝut, *see under* ȝet